POETRY

ESCAPE

LONDON

Edited By Jenni Harrison

First published in Great Britain in 2019 by:

Young Writers Est. 1991

Young Writers
Remus House
Coltsfoot Drive
Peterborough
PE2 9BF
Telephone: 01733 890066
Website: www.youngwriters.co.uk

FOREWORD

Since 1991 our aim here at Young Writers has been to encourage creativity in children and young adults and to inspire a love of the written word. Each competition is tailored to the relevant age group, hopefully giving each student the inspiration and incentive to create their own piece of creative writing, whether it's a poem or a short story. We truly believe that seeing their work in print gives students a sense of achievement and pride.

For our latest competition Poetry Escape, we challenged secondary school students to free their creativity and escape the maze of their minds using poetic techniques as their tools of navigation. They had several pathways to choose from, with each one offering either a specific theme or a writing constraint. Alternatively they could forge their own route, because there's no such thing as a dead end where imagination is concerned.

The result is an inspiring anthology full of ideas, hopes, fears and imagination, proving that creativity really does offer escape, in whatever form you need it.

We encourage young writers to express themselves and address topics that matter to them, which sometimes means exploring sensitive or difficult topics. If you have been affected by any issues raised in this book, details on where to find help can be found at: **www.youngwriters.co.uk/support.**

CONTENTS

Adam Mustafa (13) 59
Abul Hasan (13) 60
Enis Koesem (13) 62
Ismail Malik (11) 63
Huzaifa Mujahid Ali (13) 64
Hamid Alom (13) 66
Reyhad Jony (11) 67
Anwar Omar Halane (12) 68
Usman Iqbal (13) 69

Harris City Academy, Crystal Palace

Archana Navajeevan (12) 70
Sé Gerard Conaghan (11) 71
Maryam Adegbite (11) 72
Diego Cortes Merida (11) 74
Ellie Jean Paige Lawrence (11) 76
Luigi Castiglieri (11) 77
Tiania Jasime Wright (11) 78
Riya Ganger (12) 79
Muhammad Sala (11) 80
Anna-Marie Jowers (12) 81
Jaela Bircham (11) 82
Asuma Jalloh Jalloh (12) 83

Hereward House School, Hampstead

Irfan Adam Irwan Shahrin (12) 84
Tom Heinlein 86
Arun Khiani (12) 88
Hector Elwes 89
Zak Smith (11) 90
Arthur Kingscote 91
Ritchie Grant (11) 92
Leo Jagger Silverston (12) 93
Harry Hawkins (11) 94
Arthur Noble 95
Oliver Anstee (12) 96
James Mees (12) 97

International Academy Of Greenwich, Lee

Jenny Ikhatalor (13) 98
Chloe Elenam Blackmore (13) 100
Rawdon Heavens 101
Myles Swan O'Sullivan (12) 102
Libni Deodee 103
Zain Osman (14) 104
Patrick Payne (12) 105

Italia Conti Academy Of Theatre Arts, Islington

Madison Turner (11) 106

Morpeth School, Bethnal Green

Lola Baty (12) 107
Amisha Dutta (12) 108

Mulberry Academy Shoreditch, Tower Hamlets

Zaynab Ali Sultana (11) 110
Anisa Akunjee (11) 111
Hasan Ahmed (12) & Ayuub Warsama 112
Zara Rakib (11) 114
Abdishakur Yussuf (11) 116
Khadeja Nusrat (11) & Zafirah Mujahid (11) 117
Zakaria Hasan (11) & Labibah Boshor (11) 118
Inaaya Zahraa Ahmed (11) 119
Aliyah Adeyemi (11) 120
Samir Hussain (11) 121
Saffa Ahmed (11) 122
Mehreen Chowdhury (11) 123
Ericka Kasongo (11) 124
Bushra Kashemi (11) 125
Md Shafi Md Hamid (11), Farhat, Hanif & Shourov Hanif (12) 126

Zaid Zubair (12) & Waseem Ahmed (11) — 127

Mulberry UTC, Bow

Abigail Manning (15) — 128

Newman Catholic College, Brent

Salim Mohamed (15) — 130
Kurt Hans Almirez (14) — 132
Ozzy Majewski (14) — 133
Samuel Davis (14) — 134
Simeon Bozilov (14) — 136

Sedgehill School, Lewisham

Ava Annis Klara Drew (12) — 137
Shannay — 138
Javyn — 141
Chardonnay Warner Hall (14) — 142

Southfields Academy, Wandsworth

Ilinka Jevtovic (17) — 143

St James Senior Girls' School, Hammersmith

Skyla Jane Robertson (11) — 145
Stella Robinson (13) — 146
Hazel Galloway (12) — 148
Bea Wright (12) — 149
Gabriella Claire Pinheiro Boyle (12) — 150
Alice Fay Raeburn (13) — 151
Isabel Thomas (13) — 152
Isla Ivanovic (11) — 153
Alice Suppiah (12) — 154
Scarlett Jones (13) — 155
Lula Packshaw (12) — 156
Dulcie Airey-Lawrence (11) — 157
Anete Mottus (11) — 158
Rose Brabyn (11) — 159

St Matthew Academy, Blackheath

Praise Onye-Koller (11) — 160
Nickoyah Aaliyah Forrest (12) — 162
Wendy Arthur-Forson (12) — 163
Beth Chowdhury — 164
Tabi Istvan Ajuyah-Valentine (12) — 166
Kassandra Kamegni Kadji (12) — 167
Janae Daley (12) — 168
D'Metri Ramator — 169
Shemmy Abidemi Adepoju (13) — 170
Iciar Aranda Lopez (11) — 171
Nivithan Nageswaran (11) — 172
Daniella Olusanya (12) — 173
D'Angelo Pinnock (11) — 174
Kaede Takeda (11) — 175
Sami Ahmad (13) — 176
Marvel Katchisicho Ozorka (12) — 177
Ashley Thomas (11) — 178
Hugo Hernandez Muelas (13) — 179
Kavin Premkumar (12) — 180

Thames Christian School, Clapham

Mary Mullagiri (14) — 181
Bailey Bright (13) — 182
Elijah Booth (15) — 184
Max McFarlane (13) — 186
Tsion Tafari (13) — 187
Micah Donnan (14) — 188
Leilani Champagnie (13) — 189

The Ellen Wilkinson School For Girls, Acton

Chelsea Nicole Findley (13) — 190
Terriesia Blackstock (13) — 192
Raisa Khan Ahmed (13) — 193
Ada Ulusoy (13) — 194

The Royal Docks Community School, Newham

Aisha Creary (15) & Lara Marah (15)	195
Mahek Rabbani (14)	196
Adeil Glulam (11)	198
Sabina Memia (11)	199
Bianca Constantin (11)	200
Bailey Scott-Fisher (11)	201

Ursuline High School, Wimbledon

Chloe Yagoub Arostegui (12)	202
Eimear Fehily (13)	203
Chantal Badayos (12)	204
Gemma Sweeney (12)	206
Rosemary Chiamaka Ukaha (12)	207
Sophia Theresa Libera-Bennett (12)	208
Sia Bart (12)	209
Sophie Jeanine Zirps (13)	210
Lana Kirstie Howlett (12)	211
Izabella Mia Dudziec-Mabasi (13)	212
Carolina Agulhas Goncalves (13)	213
Siena Winstone (13)	214
Maya Carla Staron (12)	215
Ella Delaney (12)	216
Jessica Mae Reeves (12)	217
Katie Pryor (12)	218
Masha Nesterenko (12)	219
Eirinn Furey (13)	220
Anna Banks (12)	221
Grace Stanger (12)	222
Franchesca Sales Brosas (13)	223
Martyna Mackow (12)	224
Freya Smith (12)	225
Janaya Prempeh-Maitland (12)	226
Cliona O'Brien (12)	227
Amelia Brewster (12)	228
Isabella Brown (12)	229
Natalia Pasinska (13)	230
Rukevwe Agofure (12)	231

Liliana Carlon (12)	232
Erin Andrew (13)	233
Florence Conrad (12)	234
Sofia Maya Ferreiro (12)	235
Ivie Omorogiuwa (13)	236
Lara Recordon (12)	237

Westminster School, Westminster

Ben Heyes (13)	238
Arthur Boyce-Rodgers (14)	240
Baruch Lulsegged MacGregor (14)	241

THE POEMS

DEAR BULLY

You may think you're cool cos you call me names
And you may think I'm hurting inside
But do you really think I'm going to hide?

Lots of people look up to you
They're scared if they don't you'll turn sour.
I bet half of them think you're a bully
But when you speak to them they just cower.

You have everybody below you
Obeying your every demand
But if somebody bigger came along
You would bury your head in the sand.

You're not just a bully, but a coward,
Who's jealous of people like me
Am I really as bad as you make me feel
Or the person who you want to be?

I know I can talk to my teachers
My parents, family and friends
To tell them how you make me feel.

Mohammed Yusuf Sadiq (11)
Al-Risalah School, Wandsworth

FRIENDSHIP MATTERS

F or lifting me up when I am down

R emember all those good times we had running all over town

I pledge my trust, thy trust is mine

E very day when I have fun with you, that puts me on cloud nine

N ot once did you interrupt me (unless I was talking silly)

D istance and time can never change the bond between us

S omeone to lean on when our problems appear and make a fuss

H aving patience with me brings me up

I appreciate all the kindness you give me after all my break-ups

P eople, thank you for putting a smile on my face when I was wearing a frown

M y super shining stars

A nd remember when I was late and came unprepared

T he fun times and laughter we all shared

T hat is why you guys are my besties

E ven though I knew you took my festies

R emember that our friendship shall never end

S o I dedicate this poem to you, my true best friends.

Amidat Oshikoya (12)

Ark Greenwich Free School, Woolwich

TIME FOR ADVENTURE

She sat on her bed, ready to sleep
Then out of the blue she heard a loud beep.
Lying in bed, very confused,
She wanted to see what was on the news.
Watching TV, nothing interesting yet,
She scrolled across something that could be the best.
The book of escapists, what could happen next?
Maybe I should follow this trade of interests?
So she picked up her book, heading into her room,
The possibility of something, a window or broom.
Reading and reading, her mind was going crazy,
Should I escape? Yes. No. Maybe.
She chose to escape, "So listen up Mum, I'm going to escape
Make sure you don't wait."
So out of the window, onto the roof,
Could this be it, could she be let loose?
Exploring the parks, the houses, the trees,
She was getting tired, time to get some sleep.

Kayla Judge (11)
Ark Greenwich Free School, Woolwich

ESCAPING LIFE ITSELF

To escape life itself is the hardest mission of all.
Everyone goes through a tragedy
And tries to escape it at some point.
Some wonder if God was in the bullet that shot
Or the car that crashed into our loved ones.
Yes. He was.
But it's his way of setting a mission.
We all have a point in our lives
When we try to escape depression.
What we need to realise,
Is giving up is an even worse tragedy to face.
Everyone tries to run and escape,
But instead turn and face it, face-to-face.
God put us on this Earth,
Gave us a beating heart and a life to call our own
Escaping it does no good to anyone or anything.
Some believe they are in a race with life to succeed
The truth is you're in a race with yourself
To do the best you can possibly do.

Gonul Ali (12)
Ark Greenwich Free School, Woolwich

ESCAPE

Game
I'm yet to defeat the demons - *my* demons.
I try
But, my sword remains in its golden sheath.

Doubt
I suffocated that emotion with tears,
rolling from my eyes to the floor that represents life. Cold
and hard.

Sharp
I'm the
    broken
Fragments of the mirror.

Escaping
I am an addict
To that drug
It's abnormal.

Liberating
I won't break loose, I'm not
        free
Even the flying birds are chained to the sky.
Chaos
A pandemonium that I
fail to slip free of.

Shania Aaliyah Williams (11)
Ark Greenwich Free School, Woolwich

FIRE

The bright flicking flames
Lick at the dark night sky

The smoke flooding through the trees

It rises and rises

The blades of grass
Sparking up to ash

The heat becomes a burning sensation

It rises and rises

The eyes of terrified animals
Piercing through the dark filling smoke

Holding your breath
As you run

It's like an endless tunnel of fire and destruction

It gets bigger as you go
Getting bigger, more fierce
More dangerous

Your heart pounding
The sparks watering your eyes

Now you're really trying to escape
Escaping the fire
In you.

Erin Burrows (12)
Ark Greenwich Free School, Woolwich

FREEDOM TO FEEL

The stars shine bright
As I cower in fright
The night goes on
As the wolves sing their song.

They take away my freedom
They take away my will
I promise they will never
Take my freedom to feel.

Nights get shorter
Stars even brighter
I no longer stand in fright
That's for my freedom to feel.

Lucy Hickey (13)
Ark Greenwich Free School, Woolwich

THE TREE OF LIFE

Aren't there so many broken branches
In our family tree?
Generations below looking above,
In hopes of guidance, strength and security.

As the cold wind brushes past our roots,
And forgotten parts of history blow away.
We stop.
And think, how many of us will remain?

Now - we stand afraid,
Of what the world will bring.
So, we press pause, and ask ourselves,
Do we stay and hold on to a snapped branch?
Or do we endure the pain of releasing, and giving someone
else a chance?

As the seasons come and go,
Spring, summer, fall and snow.
New beginnings encase our minds
But will we learn to be brave enough in time?

Let's return to our first thoughts,
And gather everything we've learned,
Even though life tells our loved ones to leave,
There's not a lot of broken branches - in our family tree.

Joyce Grace Mambou (14)
Bishop Challoner Catholic Collegiate Girls' School, Tower Hamlets

FLAMING SWORD, DYING BIRD

Wolves howl in the pitch-black night,
Birds chirp in the golden day,
Everyone is happy,
Except for that one little birdy.

Blue and green all over,
Nowhere to go,
Or to live.

A flaming sword,
And a dying bird,
This poem may make you bored
But don't disrespect the little Earth.

Space and time are infinite,
Nowhere to start or to end,
Nowhere is straight,
All with a bend.

If you could live forever,
Oh how great that would be,
Until you fade away
With our little birdy.

Flaming sword,
Dying bird,

Like a rope cord,
Infinite loops until you realise,
Your life may be worthless.

Infinite loops until you realise your life is a word
Made by the universe.

Dimitri Dante Smith (13)
Bow School, Bow

THE RISING OF THE FLAG

A cloth is on the floor, tied to a pole.
Just a cloth. But it's not called a cloth.
It's called a flag; people's pride and joy are sewn into it.
It can speak. Right now it says this: "Don't look at me, I'm on the floor."
The clouds are grey, the people sad.
A man arrives to the pole and grabs a rope. He pulls it, and the flag rises.
It bellows in the wind. It speaks:
"I am returning! Rejoice, those under me."
The clouds clear and the people look up. They smile.
And finally, the piece of cloth reaches the top. It shouts!
"I am risen! The nation I represent, supreme!"
All is well once more for the people.
The flag rises in other nations. Yet it is not a flag of victory,
It is of sadness and anger. The flag can fly in its own land,
But must it fly over ours?
That is what mankind wishes to know.
That is what mankind will never know.
That is the sole duty of the flag.
Happiness, but oppression.
Love, but hatred.
That is the flag.

Teddy Chesebrough (11)
Devonshire House School, Hampstead

BEAUTIFUL

I have a secret love,
Her eyes as green as grass
Her hair as white as a dove.
She glides across the rooftops,
Dancing the night away.
I cry each and every night
Knowing she won't stay.

I have a secret love,
She warms me when I'm cold.
I wish that she would stay with me
'Til I'm grey and old.
I watch her live her life in joy
I want to run away with her
But she thinks I'm an unworthy toy.

I have a secret love,
I love her more than she's aware
We have many happy times together,
I hope she knows how much I care.
Dear secret love,
Even if you cannot love me in return,
The flame in my heart will always burn.

I love you Annabelle,
You'll always be my favourite cat.

Betty Dahl & Hafsa
Dunraven School Upper, Streatham

THE GIRL WHO HATES ME

It's not fun.
It's not fun to be sad.
This pain, this anger
Affects my soul.
They say 'sticks and stones don't break your bones'.

If that's true,
Why do I feel so weak?
Why do I feel so down?

The tears,
They fall as hard as hail,
The emotions,
They are frozen like ice,
Never melting, but frozen.

I'm the girl who cries in her room.
I'm the girl who despises her face, her body.
I'm the sensitive girl at the back of the room.
I'm the girl who hates me.

I skip lunch.
I skip dinner.
Loved ones who come, leave,
Just like that, they go, one by one.

Sometimes I wonder if the next one is me.
What if I just leave,
Leave the world?

It's not like anyone will care.
I've given up on this body I wear.

The things I hear, the things I see.
Nothing compares to the girl who hates me.

Delina Kehase
Dunraven School Upper, Streatham

EXTINCTION

On I walk

Sand crunches beneath my paws
The soft forest floor absorbs all noise.

The sun scorches my stripes.
I used to dance between the dense trees and the dappled light.

Tumbleweed rolls past me.
The luscious shrubs used to stroke my fur.

A single tree casts an eerie shadow in front of me.
I used to dart through the moist darkness of thick tree trunks.

The silence is so dry, I could crack it with my claws.
The rainforest buzzed with life, vibrating through my soul.

There is no food in sight.
I used to catch three meals a day, if I had the inclination.

Man took the rainforest from me.
I am the last tiger.

On I walk.

Precious Anjolaoluwa Olaoshebikan (13)
Dunraven School Upper, Streatham

TO A FUTURE ME

Enjoy your life
Enjoy your time
Enjoy your food
Enjoy playing in the grass
Enjoy being young and free
Enjoy being someone like me

Have some fun with the faeries
Have fun in the sun
Have fun with your teachers
Have fun with your friends
Have fun with school
Have fun in a pool.

Take passion in your sports
Take pride in yourself
Take part in something new
Take part in a club
Take part in a run
Take part in something fun

Be yourself
Be young
Be wild
Be happy
Be sad
Don't feel bad.

Imogen Fenner Scally (14)
Dunraven School Upper, Streatham

TO MY FUTURE SELF

My skin is my past
My skin is my future
My skin is my everything
Even right now

But just because it binds me
That does not mean it defines me
My skin is everything
Even right now

I love my mum
I love my dad
Even though it means
At times I am sad
Knowing that some day
They will pass away
Leaving me alone
On Earth to stay

I will love my son
My daughter
My girlfriend
My wife
My new life

I know that my future
Is far away

But my skin is my future
And it's here to stay.

Naail Khan-Brown (14)
Dunraven School Upper, Streatham

AN ODE TO SILENCE

Silence.
The absence of sound.
When the machines and engines have burnt all the fuel
Thus creating silence.

Silence.
The absence of sound.
When animals are forced out of their environment
Thus creating silence.

Silence.
The absence of sound.
When humans are slaughtered because of their race or
religion
Thus creating silence.

Silence.
The absence of sound.
When we realise we have destroyed ourselves and our
planet
The endless silence.

Rhys Froux-Leaker
Dunraven School Upper, Streatham

BOREDOM

Boredom
Tap, tap, tapping of feet.
Click, click, clicking of pens.
Sounds filling my ears

Everyone has their heads down,
Locked up in their own thoughts,
But I have none.

I look up.
I look down.
I swing my eyes across the classroom.
Nothing to inspire me here.

Silence rips through my brain like a blunt knife.
Nothing will stop time standing still.
Nothing.

So I wrote this poem.

Kitty Grace Peake (12)
Dunraven School Upper, Streatham

DEPRESSION

A smile

Is what I wear on my face every day
To school
To see my friends
To talk to my family
To go out

That smile

Is a mask that I wear every day
To cover
Sadness. Pain. Scars. Tears

I feel alone

No one understands how it feels to be inside
Your room
Crying and wondering
Who knows me?
Why am I here?

But you do it silently
So no one can hear.

Sophie Baird (13)
Dunraven School Upper, Streatham

MY HEART'S A BLANKET

Fog covers me,
When it rains I hurt.
When she thunders I break
When she meets my eye I smile.
When I smile I am filled with joy,
She is my joy
When it runs I feel tired.
When they hurt I hurt,
When she steps towards me I beat.
I'm just a blanket of all these emotions.
I am a heart.
I am a human.

Daniel Dano (13)
Dunraven School Upper, Streatham

AN ODE TO MY SKIN

My skin is beautifully dark;
I absorb all the heat and light.
My skin is my people;
My Uganda, our fight.

My skin is my mother;
Her strength and her love.
My skin is my ancestors,
Watching from above.

My skin is my armour
Protecting my inner self.
My skin is precious;
Greater than any wealth.

Ragheeb Kazibwe
Dunraven School Upper, Streatham

THE FEAR

I stepped outside.
Darkness was on me.
A sliver of the shimmering moon was the only light.
I was scared
Scared of the dark.
I ran.
And ran.
Towards the light.
I felt afraid.
Nobody around me.
Thunder struck.
Rain poured down in the night.
I dropped to the floor.
This boy was never seen again.

Richard Taratoa Stappard
Dunraven School Upper, Streatham

DEPRESSION

You are under the ocean,
The emptiness surrounds you.
As you fall deeper into it,
A darkness starts to grow,
It germinates, it spreads.
You are alone in the darkness.
There is no horizon.
Your body is weightless.
Becomes part of the water,
You drift endlessly.
Forever.
Floating away.

Rufus Hanna
Dunraven School Upper, Streatham

THE DEPRESSED

Sad face
Grey clouds
Rain falling
Loneliness
Hopelessness
Lines in her skin
Blood pumps through her
Xanax down the throat
Wishing there was hope.

Patsy McLachlan (13)
Dunraven School Upper, Streatham

A JOURNEY JUST TO STOP

The guns are blazing
The world ends.
All the soldiers do is defend
The ground which they just captured,
Their strategy has still not been mastered.

The armies are still there,
Their bullets still fly through the air,
The blood is running down in streams.
They always go back home in their dreams,
Yet the nightmares still deluge their sleep.

As they walk through the muck
They think, *it's the end, we're out of luck.*
They risk their lives every day,
They're valiant heroes in every way.
But their malnourished bodies still slow down,
Their skeletal figures bunch around.

The mass graves still reek of decay
From the many who died, not just today.
War is used to make you drop
and life is a journey just to stop.

Dhin Abdul Basit (13)
East London Science School, Bromley-By-Bow

A VENTURE

(A lipogram without the letter I)

To compose a ballad bereft of the letter 'eye'
Can be cumbersome, onerous; why even try?
What would the stakes need be? Stardom, wealth or glory?
Or just a venture that makes a good story?
Perhaps just a task for a wry educator,
Or maybe the decree of a vowel hater.
No matter the reason, the task can be managed,
To know many words, a palpable advantage.
So here reads a poem for your puzzled pleasure,
That, to my best, rhymes measure for measure.
My goal was to pen a work that deems me worthy,
And please, feel free to ask me another query.

Shah Abu-Bakr Quraishi (13)
East London Science School, Bromley-By-Bow

FIRE

Sprinting, I darted across the floor coated with blood-curdling flames,
Heart pounding like an immense drum in my sweating, shivering chest,
Knees trembling in terror at the perilous, sweltering fire dancing before my tearful eyes,
For I saw fire, blazing like torches before me,

Exits blocked, I was surrounded by substantial flare reducing everything to ash,
The corpses of loved ones scattered across the ground, cold red blood before me,
A fit of rage grew inside me, my blood boiling insanely with anger,
For I saw fire, blazing like torches before me,

Beyond the soaring ring of fire was the door, my gateway to escape,
Slowly, I mustered up the courage, bracing myself,
Like a tiger pouncing upon its prey I lunged forward charging at the scorching flames,
For I saw fire, blazing like torches before me,

I leaped across the towering fire hurling above those anguishing flames,
The pain and heat of the fire was like nothing I had known before,

The never-ending pain taking control over my body shook
and shivered in agony,
For I saw fire, blazing like torches before me,

Crawling to escape I saw the door to freedom before my
bloodshot eyes,
With the last ounce of strength I had I heaved my body as
much as I could,
But an avalanche of brick and plaster crushed me, burying
me,
For I saw fire, blazing like torches before me.

Tayyab Majeed (12)

Eltham College, Mottingham

ESCAPE FROM THE MYSTERIOUS HOUSE

I knocked on the entrance door,
It opened with a creak.
I saw cracks all over the floor,
I bent down to have a peek.

Mice were scattered all over the place,
Wasps were building their nests.
One mouse cheekily untied my shoelace,
Whilst one wasp stung my chest.

From my knees up to my feet,
I tiptoed to a different door.
My heart had an irregular beat,
Was that because of someone's snore?

I looked around the bizarre room,
And identified the shadow of a man.
He was sleeping on a broom,
Holding a copper pan!

"Hello!" screeched an unpleasant voice,
That scared the life out of me!
I definitely made the right choice,
I simply had to flee!

I sprinted back to the entrance door,
I quickly shoved it open.
I took one last look at the dark brown floor,
The house that was called Croken...

Tobias Odukomaiya (11)
Eltham College, Mottingham

IMPRISONMENT

What I'm currently trapped in is much worse than a prison,
This is as if all evil death has collided and risen.
Listen to the advice I'm about to give you,
Otherwise you might end up like me too.

When you're angry, keep it inside,
Don't be rude, don't be snide,
Don't be mean, don't be impolite,
Otherwise you're in for quite a fright.

Make sure your mind is not a cage,
Or else your whole life will change;
Death itself will come and take you away,
Your chances of surviving will be like finding a needle in a
bale of hay.

Then again, like me, you could find a way to be free,
Darkness might answer your desperate pleas.

Jack O'Donnell (12)
Eltham College, Mottingham

TRAPPED ALONE WITH NOTHING AT ALL

Trapped in a cage
The hours tick by
Wait for a year
But no reply

No entry and no escape
How in the world did I get in here?
My memory is lost; what do I do?
Stuck in here all alone

No food
No water
No company
Nor warmth

This place is deserted
Nothing at all
Just me alone
Who will know?

Haresh Kaarthighan Surrenthiran (11)
Eltham College, Mottingham

DON'T DO IT

It's harmful
You'll fall off the roller coaster of life
You're getting advice
Don't be vain
You got weed and crack,
Marijuana and cocaine,
You're still going to do it,
You're insane.

You'll weep until you can't no more
You'll cry until your eyes go sore
You think you're getting fame?
A beast will overcome you
Addiction is his name.

The more spliff
You sniff
You'll feel like falling off a cliff
By doing this
You feel like you're the best
But bestowed upon you is a test.

Sometimes it's not your fault
You grab a pill
And gulp it like a catapult
But you're going to get ill

Psychologists and doctors
Keep on telling you
"Don't sniff the big blue boo!"

It doesn't give peace.
Make a different decision.
Do it with precision.
Your mum will shout
Because you're fumbling about.

Don't you know how to respect
Your friends and family.
Because if you don't,
You should expect
Catastrophe.

Don't let drugs affect your eternal life.
If you do,
They'll only bring strife.
Always let the drug of your choice,
Be that of God's Almighty voice.
If you let God's word flow within,
No drug will make you sin.

Your choice,
Drugs or love.
If I were you,
God's love would do.

Don't do drugs.
It's like filling your body with bugs.
Some weirdos say drugs give hugs.
But they're just mugs
Who sleep on rugs.
Their brains are like slugs.
Don't turn into one of those addicted thugs.

Now, to end on the last bit,
Once again,
Don't do it!

Mohammed Ajwad Uddin (12)

HAFS Academy, Stratford

NATURAL DISASTER

Natural disasters, reckless, heartless and sad,
Eliminating people every time, no survivors,
Letting no one get out of its grasp,
It is a savage tiger eating its prey,
It is like an archer shooting an explosive projectile.

Natural disasters, reckless, heartless and sad,
Hurricanes, earthquakes, tsunamis and more,
Nobody can stop it, nobody will,
It is like an explosion, destroying anything in its path,
It is a murderer, killing its victims without a thought.

Natural disaster, reckless, heartless and sad,
Demolishing the environment, causing chaos,
Houses being eradicated, houses being restored,
It is like a person littering the whole world,
It is a slave master abusing a slave.

Natural disasters, reckless, heartless and sad,
People being positive, people forgetting about the past,
People being incautious, people being suspicious,
It is like a predator lingering for the accurate instance,
It is the sun exploding and starting the world again in a new
age.

Yaseen Hussain Miah (11)
HAFS Academy, Stratford

FEELINGS

When your feelings all come at once
Like expanding your brain
It's like throwing your life
Down the drain.

When your thoughts come to the wrong
And you go through a tunnel
Your friends will flip-flop fast when you face trouble.
so by choosing the right friends will extend and amend
the time with your good friends.

The depressing feelings all at once
are just so distressing
it makes you start repressing
forcing you from progressing.

Whenever you show an expression
it brings a weight of depression
so by making up your confessions
will give you the title of a profession.

Draining your thoughts
Just like the rain
Can especially help
When you're going through pain.

Some feelings are good
It reminds you of your childhood

But you will be sure to feel the pain
When it gets to your brain.

Hurting people's feelings
Is like dealing with the devils
So don't let your words
Up in those levels.

Imagine having no feelings
Not knowing with what you're dealing
You would be going all crazy
Acting like a baby.

Feelings are emotions
It shows you and your opinions
So be sure to be careful
And do not be dareful.

Rayhan Talukder (14)
HAFS Academy, Stratford

THE PARADISE OF JUNGLES

As I quietly strolled into the exotic jungle,
Birds hummed a sweet tune,
The gentle tall trees were soldiers bestowing protection over me,
The fresh aroma of the light, lovely water tickled my nose,
And the glory of the sun glistened greatly with light to all.

Attractive colours caught my eye,
The leaves danced as if they were waving,
The long lively arms of trees hunched over the magnificent, marvellous pool,
The trees stood firmly as high as I could see,
And the amazing attractive view comforted my heart.

The rocks sat together neighbouring the natural water,
Other rocks assembled a waterfall,
From which fresh water was fed into the shallow ends,
Fish ate with serenity and peace,
And my feet felt the warm, welcoming touch of the water.

The plants grew delightful colours on rocks,
Giving them an extraordinary exotic effect,
The green grass dangled down to the pool,
Tightly holding onto the rocks,
To make sure they didn't fall.

The soft sound of the twinkling water,
Gave ease and tranquillity to my ears,
The blend of different bright beautiful colours in the pool,
Brought amazement and calmness to my mind,
And my fascinating, stunning and unbelievable journey had
come to an end.

Ibrahim Hanif Ibn Ali (12)

HAFS Academy, Stratford

OUR PLANET'S FUTURE

The waters we have, will be drowned with oil,
There will be nothing, but rubbish in soil,
The earth is our home,
Which we soon won't be able to roam.

When cars move, the exhausts just huff,
But planting a seed causes nothing but puffs,
With the blazing heat causing ice to melt,
If only we knew how the ice felt.

In the sky there's a lot of pollution,
What our planet needs is a solution,
It won't help if we carry on to litter,
If you do, you're best off a quitter.

We are endangering ourselves and the future generation,
Not just for you, but every nation,
So, if we don't stop, and litter more,
In the end, it's us who are going to end up sore.

All the animals, from sea to sky,
It's a matter of time before they die,
Their habitats are going away, bit by bit,
Soon there will be no water, just a massive oil pit.

If we all help, and do our part,
It will be nothing but an amazing start,

Then the future will be so great,
If you don't believe me, you have just got to wait.

Thamim Islam (14)
HAFS Academy, Stratford

THE SONG OF WAR

The shark-like bombs
Ready to make Earth our tomb
The sky-blue ships
Engulfing the sphere of a planet in terror
Then arrives our liberator.

But they seem to merge with the opposing fleet
Being similar in colour
Hence unidentified by the oppressor
Why? we wonder
Then comes the answer
The answer strikes hard with a loud boom!

Earth being shaken hard,
Feeling as if it may break beneath our feet
Flashes filled the black void known as space
No visible payload hit, yet the ground still rocked
The tremors grew increasingly intense by the second
Then it hit us like a missile.

The answer was crystal clear
It would result in destruction
For the answer to be without it would be a far cry
It was at the risk that many may die
For the needs of many outweighed the needs of a few.

All it required was the pull of a trigger
The aftermath would be multiple lives lost, along with a few
stars

The muzzle was aligned with the centre of the opposing fleet
The last sound to be heard was the click of a trigger.

Abdur-Razzaq Ibn Tahir (12)
HAFS Academy, Stratford

MY BEAUTIFUL MUM AND DAD

Mum, Dad, Mum, Dad
You are my only two angels
Without you I can't see.

No matter if I switch the light on
My days always go past beneficially
As I come home you're always there,
Opening the door before me
As I step in the living room
My food is always ready for me to eat.

Every morning when I get ready,
My other angel is always ready to give me a ride to school
Every day when I finish school
Both of my lovely parents are always waiting for me outside.
When I cry,
You are there wiping my tears for me.

Mum, Dad, Mum, Dad.
You are my only two ladders
When I need something I can't reach
Without looking at you
You are always there getting it for me
You are as light as the sun
And as beautiful as the rainbow.

So what can I do for you?
As I come from school
I will buy some gifts
And when I come home,
I'll always give you a gift
A gift as light as you two are
And there's nothing better than you
Please take care of your parents.

Abdullahi Ali (13)
HAFS Academy, Stratford

GOAL!

As it arrives at his feet
He easily glides past the rest
Nobody can touch him
Simply he is the best of the best
As he goes out on a limb.

His foot is a gun
Ready to shoot on command
He pulls the trigger with ease
As the ball thunders and is about to land
The goalkeeper falls to his knees.

Against all players he is always a constant threat
If you try to tackle him it will have no effect
He is easily the most powerful in the stadium
Never falters in finding the destination: the net
As the flying ball hums.

He is always calm with the ball
His feet are never going to falter
He leaves the defenders in a complete muddle
On the pitch he is always a star
The way he plays is never dull.

As he looks back at his glory days
All that is surrounding him is silverware and gold
He remembers when people gazed at him in awe

He remembers how in the back of the net his goals would be controlled
Because he was the best footballer.

Ahmad Yusuf Patel (12)
HAFS Academy, Stratford

SWEETS

I love sweets, they're my most-liked treat
Delicious chocolate and yummy soft mints,
Strawberry laces and chocolate mazes,
From chilli to sour and sour to minty,
As sour as malic acid they taste,
Deliciously mouth-watering.

From Skittles to Hershey's
A pound I need and happiness will be found
Sweets are as delicious as food and they
Always change your mood.

Sweets come in different shapes
And sizes, large and little,
Circles and square but all shapes and sizes
Are fair.

But remember sweets make you
Hyper like vipers.
You get a sugar rush when you eat too much
Which creates a big over-exaggerated fuss
Eating sweets is a must.

Oh no!
Now I've had too much,
I don't want more as I'm feeling sick,
Lying in bed feeling tricked in my head,

All that sugar upon my hands was useless
That hint of mint still on my fingers.

Abdullah Mahmood (11)

HAFS Academy, Stratford

FEELINGS IN SIMPLE WORDS

Sadness is common
It's always from the heart's bottom
Happiness is at the top
It's a feeling none can stop.

Confidence is from the left
You should always treat it as a guest
Fear comes from the right
It mostly appears in the night.

These were all from the heart
Now let's move on to another part
The head emits rather more
I might mention three or four.

Anger is from the head's centre
If you're saying you don't have it, you're the biggest
pretender
Shyness is regularly from the back
It usually makes people stack.

Loneliness stays at the front
It makes you moody and blunt
Anxiety is uncommon
But let's not let it be forgotten.

I hope you really enjoyed this
There are still a few I did miss
But let's stay on the positive side
We covered most of them so please don't be unsatisfied.

Ibrahim Boucetta (14)

HAFS Academy, Stratford

EXPLORING

Exploring is entertaining and interesting
An endless amount of possibilities
A thrust of sensation gushes through the air
A fun and exquisite journey
Leading the impossible to possible.

There is still something out there
That will release your dreams to reality
Exploring is as unique as gold
As you gaze, your eyes will glow
There is nothing preferable to looking at forests.

Struck by the world's sensation
Nature is an inspiring glow
The sun is shining
Escorting you to new things
Making you dig deeper.

Exploring is a sign of passion
Which no one can take away
It is a gift that will illuminate you
You will climb Mount Everest
Fun, frightening, fragile.

Turning back would be a casualty
This journey is everlasting
If you carry on you are a genius

You will be more than emerald
Don't stop; this is total fun!

Hasan Shamir (12)
HAFS Academy, Stratford

FRIENDSHIP

Friendship don't leave me
You are as yellow as the shining sun
You make me satisfied and comfortable
You take away sadness and bring happiness
Oh friendship don't leave my soul
You are more precious than a diamond.

Friendship, you are precious to me
You're more bright than the shining sun
Stay with me and I will be at ease
Don't leave me or I won't be able to live
Oh friendship, keep me under your shade.

Friendship, you give me someone to talk to
You make me satisfied and comfortable
You are green as the grass and trees
You help me share my feelings
Friendship, you make me happy.

You take my darkness away
If it wasn't for you, I would be in a black cave
You give me someone to play with
You take away sadness and give me happiness
Oh friendship don't leave me.

Abdur-Rahmaan Saqib (13)
HAFS Academy, Stratford

ADVENTURE LIKE NO OTHER

Had housework but didn't bother
Wanted to go on an adventure like no other
Wanted to attain freedom and fun
Desired to go to the field and run

There were countless others like me
Pondering what the result would be
But we all had a corresponding idea to be free
To travel the world and see

We endured many troubles, some we overcame
We reminded ourselves of what would be the outcome
Then we said, "For king and country!
If we win, we'll win a bounty!" (In the grave.)

We then arranged a journey
Which lasted an eternity
We settled ourselves in narrow camps
Some were wet and some were damp

Whenever we run, some of us fall
But help never responded to their call
I understood the purpose we were there for
I also understood the true meaning of war.

Adam Mustafa (13)
HAFS Academy, Stratford

FOOTBALL

Oh football,
I love playing football
More than basketball
When I play football I feel very cool.

When I score I feel happy
When I am on the ball I am snappy
I like playing 'cause it's fun
Especially in the sun.

When I kick the ball
The keeper automatically falls
When I celebrate I jump very high
It is as I fly.

I play, I get serious
Some students get curious
I stay hydrated so I can play
My number one goal is to score every day.

When I play I feel over the moon
I fly so high like a balloon
It is really healthy
And I'm trying to get skinny.

When I hit the ball it's like a bullet
Just like the player Gullit

I love playing with my friends
But I hate it when it's time to end.

Abul Hasan (13)
HAFS Academy, Stratford

THE BREATHTAKING JUNGLE

The immense and vivid jungle
Containing surprising creatures
Huge branches that give you shade
The vibrant plants so astonishing
Which will make you feel like home.

The massive and well-built trees
With enormous and radiant leaves
Their roots as powerful as gorillas
Ready to survive and storm
All of a sudden the branch snaps.

The cool wind blowing across the jungle
It then slowly starts to rain
Lightning and thunder looking like spears
Ready to penetrate through anything
Everything changes from amazing to terrifying.

The creatures all looking for shade
Different types of creatures running everywhere
Short and tall, big and small, fast and slow
Every animal following the flow
Looking like they are having their own little show.

Enis Koesem (13)
HAFS Academy, Stratford

LIFE ON MARS

An idea said to be unachievable years ago,
Came true years ago yet no one knew,
As random as rain comes, air appeared above Mars,
After evidence was found by satellites.

America blasted rockets like a towering inferno of flame.
Letting no one seize the idea,
It rushed to conquer it like a king selfish for more land,
As they landed they rushed outside without astronaut
costumes,
But with strengthened exo suits instead,
All of them poured out of the rockets like sand.

They started building with planning more advanced than
ever before,
Never before was it seen,
The darkness of the harmful side of people,
Soon fighting began as no one could go to Mars,
So it became as deserted as the deep water,
But deep below Mars, undisturbed, roamed aliens.

Ismail Malik (11)
HAFS Academy, Stratford

MY FUTURE

The future:
Will it be like a mountain of peace?
Or a disaster: crimes
Will it be free?
The future is the unseen.

My future, will I be healthy?
Will I be lonely or
Will I be wealthy?
Will I even be alive?
Will my parents be deprived?
Future, only you can decide.

Will there be flying cars
Or will we even be riding stars?
Will we live on the marvellous Mars?
Will there still be wars, leaving
People with bruises and scars?

Or will we all stand strong?
Unity and peace; the group
We all should belong
Together we will be brave and bold
What will the future hold?

Will the future be ever so bright
Or so dark, leaving us in fright?

No one will know
We just have to wait to find the untold.

Huzaifa Mujahid Ali (13)
HAFS Academy, Stratford

THE WORLD

Oh world,
Sometimes there are pleasing things
Sometimes there are dangerous things
The world was once about peace
But now that's history
Which contains a lot of controversy.

The world, what has it become?
When was the time the world had fun?
One diss here, one cuss there
People are trying to get attention everywhere
The Internet invaded the world.

The government are greedy goblins
People are earning big money
For family and their future
But that gets taken away from them because of tax.

Oh world,
What has it become?
Some are dying, others tryna run
I wish the world was back in its place
The time where kids were easy to raise.

Hamid Alom (13)
HAFS Academy, Stratford

HAPPINESS

Happiness is like
the shining blue diamond.
It makes you enjoy
the pleasing freedom.
Happiness is sipping on tea on a rainy day.

Happiness occurs
when darkness falls and brightness rises.
Happiness is like
the sign of friendship.
Happiness is the tasty chocolate bar.

Happiness here, happiness there,
we're a colourful rainbow everywhere.
If there's happiness in your heart,
your darkness will break apart.
Happiness is as fun as a funfair.

Leave the darkness
and come to the brightness.
That will bring you to the world
as colourful as LegoLand.
Happiness will never meet an end.

Reyhad Jony (11)
HAFS Academy, Stratford

FORTNITE IS KIND OF THE BEST...

Fortnite is the best
In the morning I do it before I get dressed
And I sometimes I even think it's better than tests
It's so exciting
That it makes you sit there biting
On your lip till it is purple.

Although the thing I hate
Is that the game is quite hypnotic
It is like it draws you in closer and closer
With your brain shouting at the same time, *Stop! Stop!*
But the game is drowning out that sound.

But on the other hand
Everybody plays it, even my friends
And my friends say that it is a trend
And I only play on the weekends
So I guess there is no happy end.

Anwar Omar Halane (12)
HAFS Academy, Stratford

ANGER

Like molten lava
It corrupts your mind with doubts
Steaming hot inside you
The fumes of anger blast out

A clash of fear, hurt and rage
A feeling of madness, emptiness and pain
Contempt erupts through your veins
Makes you become insane

You want to throw things
Lie down, pound and flail
Rant, rave and tantrum
Deafen the world with your wail

Anger is very consuming
And doesn't hesitate to desist
From destroying hope and joy
In its haze of red mist.

Usman Iqbal (13)
HAFS Academy, Stratford

WHAT'S YOUR NAME?

I used to imagine
I was a superhero, who could save the world
Embracing my inner euphoria.
I jumped around, bouncing to the sky
Wasn't afraid of anything
As it was my innocent childhood dream.

The world became against me
Like I wasn't wanted anymore
No one called out my name.
Neither did I.
My heart stopped, my eyes closed shut
Covered my face with a mask, there I lost my name.

A luminous voice which I clearly heard inside me
Powering up my visuals to my future.
I could hear vague heartbeat become crystal clear.
As I opened my eyes leading to a path to loving myself
Here I stood with all my faults and mistakes
Ready to face my fears.

The world has shown me I have reasons to love myself
I'll answer with my breath and my path
My name is Archana.
I am the superhero who will save the world
And embrace my inner euphoria.

Archana Navajeevan (12)
Harris City Academy, Crystal Palace

THE FUTURE: WE CAN CHANGE

The future! We're finally here,
No more trees, coal or beer,
Instead of water we have juice,
Instead of food, chocolate mousse,
You may have thought the future was a dream,
Unfortunately, it's the opposite it seems,
The world is slowly dying,
People mourning, people crying,
No one knows how to stop the war,
Nothing left, no open doors,
I think it's time to say goodbye,
We may all suffer, we may all die.

Bombs exploding everywhere,
Houses burning, no one cares,
Planes are falling from the sky,
What have we done? My oh my,
Terrorists all on the road,
At any moment they could explode,
Coral reefs all white and grey,
Goodbye my world, there's only one day.

Don't let this happen to us
We can change.

Sé Gerard Conaghan (11)
Harris City Academy, Crystal Palace

INNER FEELINGS

Mother and Father are doing it again
Feel like my life has repeated then

Argue, argue
Who are you?
Glass shattered
I questioned, "What is the matter?"

My life is terrible, sometimes I wish I was dead
I plead
Please
"Leave Mum at ease."

Why did Mum choose Dad as her groom?
My heart was blue
I felt like crying, but I had to be strong
I needed to bite my tongue

The house was already in doom
I watched everything too
Blood dripped one step at a time
Someone give me a sign

My tears were running, a shiver crept down my spine
My mum is my bloodline.

I knew my life would be over
My eyes blurred

Collapsed onto the floor
My parents were shook to the core

Inner feelings are hard to control
Telling people is your goal.

Maryam Adegbite (11)
Harris City Academy, Crystal Palace

BARS

Behind pure silver bars
I hear screams and cries
While I am here
I place my crooked ear
Next to the hundred-year-old wall
I hear conversation
While I feel a drip of water
Going through the process of condensation
Suddenly I hear a lock click
I look up
An old person with a tray
Full of rank food
I wish I could escape
Suddenly the old man disappears
The door left open
I think for a second
I get up from my wooden bed
Climbing out of the wooden structure
I run
I see what is a downhill slope
Mistaken am I
Falling fast
Hit by a branch
Holding on
Realising there is no point
The branch breaking

The branch falling with me
Down, descending
Metres from the ground
Death.

Diego Cortes Merida (11)
Harris City Academy, Crystal Palace

AUTUMN

Leaves fall, few colours
Golden leaves litter the floor
Trees start to look bare

Trees sway like the wind
Gold outlined leaves on the floor
Leaves swish on the ground

It starts to get cold
Start to prepare for winter
Snow will be here soon

It starts to get dark
It feels like days are longer
I have to be warm

Will it snow this year?
Hat, scarf, gloves all on again
It's freezing, help me

I need to get warm
I start to feel unwell now
Why? I need to sleep.

Ellie Jean Paige Lawrence (11)
Harris City Academy, Crystal Palace

ADVENTURE TIME!

Stomping through the leaves
The jungle all silent
Animals lurking through the trees
Waterdrops start to drip

Climbing up high
Reaching for the stars
How wonderful they are
The wind brushing against my face

Flying high in the sky
As I glide through the wind
Soaring like a bird
Feeling free

I wake to the sound of singing birds
Calling me to join them
Soaring across the vast open sky
I'm having a wonderful time

This is what I call adventure!

Luigi Castiglieri (11)
Harris City Academy, Crystal Palace

BEST TEACHERS

Some teachers are kind
Some teachers are scary
But they all know right
They want the best for us
You can have funny teachers
And you can have mean teachers
But you should like them all
Teachers are always here for you
When you're in trouble you can go to them
When you need help
You can go to them
So don't you fear the teachers here
Many people hate the teachers
But they are the ones
Who help you to pass your GCSEs and your SATs
This is my poem all about teachers.

Tiania Jasime Wright (11)
Harris City Academy, Crystal Palace

SPACE

Wonders around the galaxy
Splurges of unicorn vomit
In all its glory, not a single sound
Ghost quiet.
Just the eerie feeling like something's unexpected...
Bang!

You take your last breath
In awe you gaze at the luminous balls of planets
Mercury, Venus, Earth, Mars, Jupiter, Saturn, Uranus, Neptune
The colours, shapes, feelings
Doesn't it satisfy you?

No worries.
Calm.
Peace.
Hypnotised by everything!

Riya Ganger (12)
Harris City Academy, Crystal Palace

THE WORLD OF ROLLER COASTERS

Twisting and turning left, right and centre,
Hands in the air like they want to surrender
Slowly going up the peak
Whilst their bodies get weak
Going down as fast as lightning
Every second it gets more frightening
Faster and faster
The travelling of laughter
Continent to continent
Country by country
City to city
Town to town
Finally back around through the loops
Straight back to the beginning.

Muhammad Sala (11)
Harris City Academy, Crystal Palace

LOST

Silence, quick, nothing
I start to hear my breath
I'm still running
Running from my death.

Desperately trying to escape
My eyes are feeling heavy
But then I see a shape
I'm trying to keep steady.

Thud. I drop to the ground
My sight is a blur
Finally I hear no sound
I know I am finished, finished for sure.

Anna-Marie Jowers (12)
Harris City Academy, Crystal Palace

AUTUMN SEASON

Honey-coloured leaves falling from trees
Crisp apples falling from the trees
Or being plucked for silky, warm apple cider
Salty sweetness of pumpkin engulfed
In a golden pastry case
With a sweet and salty crunch
Trees change colour
Letting the leaves go.
This is autumn
Enjoy it
Before wonderful winter.

Jaela Bircham (11)
Harris City Academy, Crystal Palace

LOST OR FOUND?

I wake up feeling hypnotised
I don't know what to do
My grandmother's grave feels cold
Tears dripping on her

I take my last kiss, bye
What will I do?
No brothers, sisters, mum, dad
All by myself.

Asuma Jalloh Jalloh (12)
Harris City Academy, Crystal Palace

THE THIRD WORLD WAR

The world experiences a crazy battle,
Between countries raging like a stampede of cattle,
When leaders from Korea go against the United States,
Up go all the death rates.

Millions, or even billions of people perish,
And it might seem like the population will vanish,
Many homes and families are lost,
For this is what a crazy world war will cost.

Even more to add to this destruction and crisis,
Are the terrorist groups and forces of ISIS,
Many people are still disputing,
Whether it was started by Trump or Putin.

The religious say that this is God's call,
And all of Satan's workers will fall,
But how could this be,
If many of the dead are babies that cry,
And innocent children and mothers die?

The fathers (and some mothers) go to fight,
But many never live to see the next day's sunlight,
Mothers flee to safety to ensure the family survives,
While the soldiers lose their lives.

After a decade, the United States were down,
And North Korea were the champions and took the crown,

At least four billion people were slain,
And the world had to rebuild Earth again.

They went through all the torture, all the pain,
Acting like animals, going inhumane,
Just because of one argument, one stupid fight,
To cause such chaos and for ten years, no delight!

After another fifteen years of work, they made it the same,
With North Korea having lots of fame,
This shows war is caused just by one little thing,
Making the winner the world's new king.

Irfan Adam Irwan Shahrin (12)
Hereward House School, Hampstead

PERSEUS

Of the many Greek tales
This is of a hero bold
Zeus' son Perseus

In the state Argos
The evil king has no son
The king wants an heir

He has an idea
He goes to the oracle
It gives bad news

The king is very scared
His daughter's child will kill him
He jails the princess

A baby is born
It's named Perseus
The king finds out

The king is worried
But the king throws them to sea
In a wooden box

They land on an isle
It is called Seriphos
They stay for many years

Then he is tricked
He must kill Medusa
With only sixteen

It's impossible
Medusa is a gorgon
Her eyes turn to stone

He can't look at her
His father now helps him out
He gets a mirror

Now he can see too
He creeps up on Medusa
He swings the sharp sword

The head separates
Blood gushes out of the wound
Medusa is slain.

Tom Heinlein
Hereward House School, Hampstead

NAMASTÉ

It may be the smell of the spices,
It may be the people who live there,
It may be the language and culture,
It may be the temples and prayers.

It may be the smell of the spices,
That tell you you've arrived,
It may be the scent that tickles your nose,
And makes you dream of the food you will eat.

It may be the people who live there,
That tell you you've arrived,
It may be the glistening bangles and saris,
Made of wonderful sequins and silk.

It may be the language and culture,
That tells you you've arrived,
It may be the camels and cows,
Roaming the crowded streets.

It may be the incense and prayers,
That tell you you've arrived,
It may be the beautiful temples and mosques,
Echoing a call to prayer.

Arun Khiani (12)
Hereward House School, Hampstead

ODE TO OUIJA

Black letters lie upon your face,
Bring peril to the human race
The wood of which you are but made
Has made the strongest men afraid
When the living question you
You answer them with just the truth
The sun that shines next to the 'Yes'
The light of which the heavens bless
Does send its light long ways to go
Across the board to the moon of 'No'
This moon reflects the sun's great light
Around the board all shining white
The planchette, moved by mortals of disgrace
Asks you questions in all good grace
You answer them so truthfully
You leave them going cheerfully
But those who do not say goodbye,
You know, for them, the end is nigh.

Hector Elwes
Hereward House School, Hampstead

CANCER...

The doctor said I had cancer and there was nothing he could do.
He told me go out and enjoy life but how could you when you knew...
How would you feel if everything stopped and darkness ruled the day
And there was nothing you could do...
You would feel distraught, wouldn't you?
Cancer is like an army destroying all it sees
Ruining lives one by one, but it is still looking for another.
Cancer is like torture, it destroys your body, heart and soul, cell by cell, inch by inch.
Every second becomes an hour, every hour becomes a day
And all you want is an end
A nice, peaceful end.

Zak Smith (11)
Hereward House School, Hampstead

AN ODE TO WALES

The beautiful countryside of virescent green,
The whisky clouds cover the desolate sky above.
The leaves in their suits of amber and gold,
Dance to the leaden mud underfoot.

The aromatic trees marked the path,
Creatures called beyond the thick wall of nettles and brambles.
Small white specks covered the fields
Like cotton buds grazing on the luscious grass.

The rain descended from the lead-coloured clouds,
People rushed to take shelter from the small pellets.
The fire was roaring vigorously spitting small embers,
Everyone was sat around the cosy fire.

Arthur Kingscote
Hereward House School, Hampstead

STEPPING OUT THERE

As I tie my special boots
I quickly think to myself, what do I really do?
Do I score bundles of goals like a top Ballon d'Or striker?
Or do I bowl out the best batsman like a fearsome tiger?
Do I win grand slam titles like Murray?
Or do I play like Steph Curry?
Do I break world records like Bolt?
Or am I the best American swimmer like Phelps?
Have I retired like Stevie G?
Or do I still bang in goals like Griezzy?
This is the end of my sporting career
But I'll still be on MOTD like Shearer.

Ritchie Grant (11)
Hereward House School, Hampstead

EQUALITY

Why do we treat one better than another?
Is being fair really such a bother?
To save your face? Is that true?
That's why we need to talk to you.

The pay gap is enough
So why make them feel so rough?
The workplace is supposed to have equality
But that is not the reality.

We can only try to persuade you
But we cannot change you
We need to spread our voice
So you can make an important choice
It is down to you
What will you do?

Leo Jagger Silverston (12)
Hereward House School, Hampstead

THE FUTURE

The future is a dangerous place
Nations competing to win the technology race.

Soldiers running into battle
A common sound is the machine-gun rattle

Families hiding underground
Listening for any sound

Animals and nature could not last
They died out long ago, deep in the past...

Death and destruction is everywhere
Hope is lost in evil's lair

All this could be averted
If to our planet we are alerted.

Harry Hawkins (11)
Hereward House School, Hampstead

DEVASTATION

The trees swayed,
the moonlight shone,
what was laid in the glade
was hopefully gone.

The wind rushed past
in the gleaming light -
we would have to be fast
to last the night.

The trees' masts broke,
while everything was shadowed
by night's great cloak.
Foul things crept,
while nothing good slept.

Reckless ruin, devious hate,
these terrible things were served
on a cold lead plate.

Mercenaries vapid,
tranquillity distraught.
The chase was rapid,
my muscles taut.

Arthur Noble
Hereward House School, Hampstead

CYBERBULLY

What is it that I have done to you
That makes you do the things you do?

I only want to be your friend
But your hateful words they offend

What you write is so abusive
Acidic messages that are so corrosive

I feel alone and hurt inside
An abandoned dog left on the roadside

I no longer want to be at school
And face more jabs and ridicule

The person I was has gone inside
There is no one that I can confide

How can I stand up to popularity
When I am the minority?

Oliver Anstee (12)
Hereward House School, Hampstead

MY MOTHER

Let me talk to you about my mum,
Whose brilliance is hard to sum.
Her home state is Queensland,
Where she sunbathes on the sand.
She's very social,
To everyone she is a local.
She is the nicest woman I know,
At kindness she is a pro.
Her age is forty-seven,
And she represents Heaven.
She also represents a dove,
And she is my mum who I love.

James Mees (12)
Hereward House School, Hampstead

NOWADAYS

Gang signs and knife crimes,
All happening at the same time,
No one gives a chance for us to explain,
As we don't know how to express our pain,

We are judged; a misconception
They see us on TV - the news
They are hurt for the way we have become as a generation,
Crying, laughing - then they realise,
These are *our* children

Bang! Argh!
Someone drops,
All in awe,
Another disastrous event,
Leaving a family in tears that will never be whole again,

We live,
We die,
No one remembers our past,
The fun, energetic kids we once were,
Are all forgotten,
"What happened to us?" a lady says.
We're on the road and you hear us cursing,
"How can we just say that to each other?" they say
We learn we are a world of our generation,
So, let us not end up at the station.

Our generation needs your support,
A place we can express,
Our highs, our lows,
Selling out our sins to the holy ghost,
They wait for the truth to unfold...

Jenny Ikhatalor (13)
International Academy Of Greenwich, Lee

BANG, BANG, BANG

Shots are fired,
And then the person runs.

They laugh at the misery they have caused,
At the life they paused.

Halfway,
In the grey
The dead lie on the floor,
With a life they did not have before,
When the family gets called
And has the call of their life.

Your son is dead.

Family crying for
The loss of their child,
The child that has been exiled.

Only an innocent,
Not indifferent,
But ends up dead.

The family copes with the loss,
As they walk across,
The aisle of their dead son's funeral,
As they now know they will never be whole again,
As they cry in vain.

Chloe Elenam Blackmore (13)
International Academy Of Greenwich, Lee

I DON'T RIDE A BROOMSTICK

Our skin is not green, wrinkled or cracked.
We don't ride a broomstick.
With a majestic black cat.
We treasure love.
We treasure nature.
We respect all.
We live forever.

We are Wiccans.
We are not haters.
We care for all.
We worship nature.

It's the end of the ode.
Just remember this.
All us witches.
Live by the code.

An' ye harm none,
Do as ye will.

Rawdon Heavens
International Academy Of Greenwich, Lee

BILL THE SLOTH

(Haiku poetry)

On the island beach
In the sunlight of autumn
The mountain core stirs

Bill the sloth watches
The distant sky. As the dark
Volcano explodes

He stares at his home
The sky burns, the country dies
But Bill, he survives

He rides a heron
Time stops, the ocean flows by
Ahead, Bill sights land.

They land on the shores
His old world is gone. But his
New life does begin.

Myles Swan O'Sullivan (12)
International Academy Of Greenwich, Lee

LIFE

As I stay in a world with happiness
There is still struggle.
Life is a gift to send
Life is a gift for God to end.

Life is a puzzle
Life is a puzzle
Sometimes it is tough
Sometimes it is simple.

I did not come into the world
To prove anything,
I came into this world
To love everyone.

Libni Deodee
International Academy Of Greenwich, Lee

ON BOARD

(Haiku poetry)

In the summer heat
A family gets on board
Their life is no more

The ship sounds its horns
Finally, they have arrived
In their new homeland

Kicked out to the streets
The Windrush generation
Do not have a home.

Zain Osman (14)
International Academy Of Greenwich, Lee

MONDAY

(Haiku poetry)

I stood on the edge
Feeling the bite; winter night
I let go, I fly

The wind was blowing
My hair was raising backwards
I knew this was it

I could see the brick
I was very close to it
Goodbye, senseless world.

Patrick Payne (12)
International Academy Of Greenwich, Lee

SOMETIMES...

Sometimes I wake up late
Sometimes I text a mate
Sometimes I eat on the go
And sometimes I eat very slow

Sometimes I am stressed
Sometimes I feel the best
Sometimes work is a struggle
And it gets me in a muddle

Sometimes I forget
Sometimes I am ready and set
Sometimes I miss my train
And then I go home again

Sometimes there is traffic
Sometimes I watch a film about magic
Sometimes I feel supernova
And finally my day is over.

Madison Turner (11)
Italia Conti Academy Of Theatre Arts, Islington

SO FAR YET SO CLOSE

The waves are crashing like the storm in my head
I just need to remember the words that Ma said
I feel so alone on this crowded boat,
Remembering her voice brings a lump in my throat
"You'll be okay,
Just remember this day,
I love you so much."
And she reached out to touch,
My scared little face
My life can't be a waste,
And she's been gone,
For now so long,
While I'm here,
Full of fear.
When the men came,
Each with a knife
She sacrificed herself to save my life.

Lola Baty (12)
Morpeth School, Bethnal Green

BEDTIME ESCAPE

It's time for bed,
My mum said,
She turned off the light,
Then disappeared out of my sight,
It struck 9pm on the clock,
The only words that seeped into my room were 'tick tock'
I did not want to close my eyes,
And wait for the morning sunrise,
As I was on an empty stomach,
I was craving for something to eat,
So I got down from bed and tiptoed on my feet,
Then my tummy began to growl and groan, yearning
Wishing that my mum would not hear,
For me it was concerning,
I snuck downstairs and past the living room, into the kitchen
I saw a huge silver fridge, which
Was in the corner of the area, waiting for me,
To grab something, without giving it a fee,
As I opened the fridge, an icy-cold breeze,
Swept all over me
The first thing I saw was a block of cheese,
I scanned inside the fridge until something caught my eye,
I saw a slice of chocolate cake
As I could not cook
It was something that I did not have to bake or fry,
I reached out for it and took a bite,

As I turned around,
I saw a female shadowy figure in my sight,
Uh-oh. I knew I was done for,
As I saw my mum entering with a quiet roar,
My mistake, she was only yawning,
Then she had her eyes directly looking at me, calling
Out my name but it did not turn out so bad for me, for sure,
As she was not shouting or yelling as she is pure,
The moral of today's poem is to never sneak out
Or do anything without your parents' permission,
You need to think if what you are doing
Is right or wrong
Always make the right decision!

Amisha Dutta (12)
Morpeth School, Bethnal Green

ME AND MY BROTHER

There used to be three: Mum, Dad and me
Until there's another, my new baby brother.
My baby brother's name is Joe,
I can't wait for him to grow.
As Mum is feeding Joe,
Don't know if my feeling is known.
He cries in the night and sleeps in the day,
He has no idea of how to play.
While I like to cook
My baby brother likes to read his book.
He screams so loud, which makes him proud.
I look at my brother, all I see is my mother.
He has a frown which reminds Dad of wearing a crown.
Mother gives my brother all the bunnies
While I get all the monies.
Now that he has grown
He is the king of the throne,
But still all he does is moan.
He gets all the attention, all I get is detention.
We play in the park but need to get home before dark.
He is very giving, however, I am more forgiving.
We mostly have fun in the sun.
I come to realise I love my baby brother
And I can't wait for my mum and dad to have another...

Zaynab Ali Sultana (11)
Mulberry Academy Shoreditch, Tower Hamlets

A BETTER LIFE

I woke up
Staring into the darkness
My family by my side
Ready to escape from the heartless
Our bags full of clothes
All neat, ready in rows
Tomorrow we'll be on the other side of the world.

Cold with only one thin blanket
My two brothers on the side
They cried and cried
My two sisters on the other
They slept and slept
While I was worrying about
What was going to happen next.

After a few hours
We are still on water
Being away from home
Is like being tortured
But we are here for a better life
With no wars or fights
So let's appreciate what we've got
People might think we don't have a lot
But we are here for a better life
With no wars or no fights.

Anisa Akunjee (11)
Mulberry Academy Shoreditch, Tower Hamlets

THE FUTURE

The future is full of war
People dying everywhere
Devastation, tears and gore
Worldwide murder
Innocents are killed
They die because of hunger
No one can take it any longer
No one can take it any longer
No one can live in a world of war!
There will be peace is what they swore
But what happens when the world is no more?

Is it bad or good?
The future is a mystery
It's covered with a hood
Bombs could be flying
The future is like history
People could be screaming
While they are fleeing
Or, life can be wonderful
The future is a mystery
The future can be bountiful
The future can change history
There are many decisions
You can choose
You can change the world's conditions.

Calm and quiet the world continues
Worldwide peace; everyone agreeing
Helpful and kind, the world continues
The world is finally seeing
Happiness is filling
Life is accepted
Now not rejected!

Hasan Ahmed (12) & Ayuub Warsama

Mulberry Academy Shoreditch, Tower Hamlets

A MYSTERY WORLD

The portal opened as it rained
And we walked in front to see it claim
Who will go into the torture
Sadly it was me
I walked in and saw the water
The poison water, the deadly sea
The deadliest shark there could be.

I wandered past the danger
Pretending to sneak like a Power Ranger
I ran and saw the same thing
But this time with more bling
The shiny water, the golden sea
The sparkliest shark there could be.

I ran again to see what was next
I screamed as I saw a big T-rex
I ran and ran until I lost him
Then I saw it again
This time it was more like a bin
The dirty water, the smelly sea
The most vomiting shark there could be.

I walked slowly to the light
It got more and more, just as bright
Then I saw the worst of torture
I walked in and saw my friends in the water

Drowning in the water, in the polluted sea
Getting eaten by the deadliest shark there could be.

Zara Rakib (11)

Mulberry Academy Shoreditch, Tower Hamlets

MURUGO

Somalia is in a struggle
Somalis are separating themselves
Civilians dying
Drowning in the sea
Or killed in fighting
Militants or civilians
Soldiers or pirates
They are still people.

Somalis are killing our country
Northerners - southerners
Somalilander - Somalians
We are still Somalis.

We are dividing ourselves into tribes
Isaaq - Darod
Hawiye - Rahanweyn
Why are we?

We have the same culture
We have the same religion
But we hate each other
Why do we?

Abdishakur Yussuf (11)
Mulberry Academy Shoreditch, Tower Hamlets

THE CABIN

Walking along the gravel path,
The moon shining brightly across the riverside,
Stepping through dark to light,
Only to find an abandoned cabin,
Owls spoke their own language,
Wolves howled from behind me,
Soon the door creaked open just for me,
Nobody seemed to be inside,
I tiptoed in and then I knew a mistake had been made,
I looked around the wooden house,
Nobody was there, or so I thought,
Then I took one step more,
Suddenly I was pinned to the ground,
Now I know I was never to be found.

Khadeja Nusrat (11) & Zafirah Mujahid (11)
Mulberry Academy Shoreditch, Tower Hamlets

THE NEW PLANET

Walking across an unknown floor
I hear a sound as if calling to me
I lie gazing at the infinite row of stars
I feel as if I am in a never-ending sleep
Looking up at the night sky
Wondering how I got here and where I am
No one to see or hear
But only the whistling of gravity
Nothing to interact with but the red floor
I gaze up to the sky again
I scream as loud as I can
My voice aching but calm
I cannot understand the reason why
Another day has now flown by.

Zakaria Hasan (11) & Labibah Boshor (11)
Mulberry Academy Shoreditch, Tower Hamlets

SPACE

Space is all around us, sometimes we get lost.
When we are lost in time, and you feel like a mime,
Free in space and time.
Space is like a race, which has us leaving a trace.
It's like a case full of secrets with a note écrite
Personal space we all have, like the spikes of an agave
Long and never-ending outer space
Just like our staircase
Real space is great, like a first mate.
Space is the best, like true feelings expressed!

Inaaya Zahraa Ahmed (11)
Mulberry Academy Shoreditch, Tower Hamlets

TRUE BEAUTY

When you come home from a long day at work
Remove that make-up, it can't hurt
Stare in the mirror and see true beauty
And wash off that perfume that smells oh so fruity
All you can do is wonder why people hide their true self
So elegant and pretty you could just melt
So come on people, no need to fake
Just tell the truth with no mistakes
All we have to do is give what you take
Then do it all again when you wake.

Aliyah Adeyemi (11)
Mulberry Academy Shoreditch, Tower Hamlets

WHAT'S THE WEATHER TODAY?

(Haiku poetry)

Winter:
The wind howls at you
A blizzard swirls up and down
Fun snowball fighting.

Spring:
Slushy ice and snow
Trees regain their leaves and buds
Beautiful buds grow

Summer:
Beautiful flowers
It is great to have ice cream
Fun sunny days out

Autumn:
Trees are almost bare
Colourful leaves blow away
Outside getting cold.

Samir Hussain (11)
Mulberry Academy Shoreditch, Tower Hamlets

THE FUTURE WILL COME

In the future I wish to be a doctor
Some futures are good and some are bad
But whatever you do, you still try
When the future comes,
Some people will live and some will die
Every minute, every second depends on our future lives
Even if you're sad you should be glad
Because all the moments of our lives
Makes new memories
And makes us smile.

Saffa Ahmed (11)
Mulberry Academy Shoreditch, Tower Hamlets

WHEN I FEEL CALM

P eaceful is reading books
E xciting when my friends and family come
A mazed when I get good grades
C olourful reminds me of a rainbow
E xcited when there's a holiday
F riends will be forever, no matter what happens
U nfortunately I forgot my homework
L aughing joyfully with my friends.

Mehreen Chowdhury (11)
Mulberry Academy Shoreditch, Tower Hamlets

LOOKING AT MY FUTURE SELF

Reaching the future
I'm looking down at myself
Seeing how I struggle
No money for the children
Look at how they cry
In a cold, dark apartment
Wishing I listened
To my poor old mum and dad
I need to behave
I need to have a good life
I'm running back home
I need to change the future.

Ericka Kasongo (11)
Mulberry Academy Shoreditch, Tower Hamlets

MYSTERIOUS ODE

Oh mysterious creature
We come to play hide-and-seek
But once we leave
You shall never peek.

We travel from land and sea
To see where we will be

No matter where we go
We will always flow

We travel through the darkening sky
As I marvel, you pass me by.

Bushra Kashemi (11)
Mulberry Academy Shoreditch, Tower Hamlets

THE LIFE OF US

The life of us is important to us
We have fun, that is why we run
We trust each other with each other
Time to time we have extraordinary adventures
Our lives are important to us.
We escaped from the devil's nest
Now our days are full of fun
Sadly the end has come.

Md Shafi Md Hamid (11), Farhat, Hanif & Shourov Hanif (12)
Mulberry Academy Shoreditch, Tower Hamlets

THE FUTURE OF TECH

The future is bright
Phones, games and other delights
Entertain ourselves
New generation
Don't forget the PlayStations
New Lamborghinis
Planes from different countries
Games are more real
It is really surreal.

Zaid Zubair (12) & Waseem Ahmed (11)
Mulberry Academy Shoreditch, Tower Hamlets

SHADOWS

I remained in your shadow
buried in woe
hidden from light and all things aglow
behind closed doors handcuffed with spirit low.
For every chance at freedom blown further than the wind
could throw.
For I was in your shadow.

They said I reflected you
I then shaved my appearance.
They say I'm just like you
how I have your perseverance
and ability to thrive after Daddy's disappearance.
How despite my losses and woe
I was 'free'
and able to let our binding creativity flow.
But behind those doors that you don't know
I was handcuffed with spirit low
and every hope for freedom blown further than the wind
could throw.
For I was in your shadow.

My desire to break free
shows I'm not some silhouette
but Abbey
is broken in this reality
as I continue to be associated with selfishness and horrid
mentality

the thought pattern a brutality.
Yet.
I do not speak out with any opposition
I worthlessly communicate wordlessly
for they do love whose colours are just revealed to me.
Hidden in the dark places they do not know that truth in the face they see
and say one day it'll be me.
The possibility deflecting joy's invasion
shielding me from happiness' vulnerability.
My voice - an echo
unable to penetrate these boundaries
defining restrictions confine me.

Abigail Manning (15)

Mulberry UTC, Bow

UNCERTAINTY LYING AHEAD

The future, it looks so bright
Too much to even see
The future, it's beginning to dim its light
Nothing is a guarantee

The future, an unachievable dream
Yet believed to be reality
The future, yet to show itself
But still followed, unfortunately

The future, it paralyses the unprepared
It leads to failure
The future, still undeclared
Prowling for it, human behaviour

The future, filled with uncertainty
Pushing you forward to do your best
The future, drawing creativity
To be expressed

The future can be anything
However, the choice is out of sight
The future, no point in worshipping
You may never get out of your plight

The future, it eventually stops
However, only for you
The future, surprising you with what it drops
Not even giving you a clue.

Salim Mohamed (15)
Newman Catholic College, Brent

I'M REALLY HAPPY, I SWEAR...

I am the chosen one
First, allow me to breathe and let the lie be pride
Let the wind take away the anxiety inside me and let it be none
Secondly, take off the fear inside
Allow my heart to agree so I don't die
Show me the way, where the sun meets the sea
Where the moon kisses the sky
Please carry the emotion that you brought me and let it be free
Thirdly, lie to the feeling I've shown you
I know it doesn't make any sense,
But it doesn't have to make sense
I'm sorry I can't help you, but at least give me a clue
I can't handle the earnestness so I let the air defense
Block the intensity that's controlling over my mind and never have fun.
Lastly, let me escape from being the chosen one.

Kurt Hans Almirez (14)
Newman Catholic College, Brent

LIPOGRAPH: WITHOUT THE 14TH LETTER

The 14th letter of the alphabet has disappeared
Chaos as people try to spell words with that letter
People flustered, why is there a bare key at my keyboard?
The leaders of our 'glorious' territory are evil
Robots tasked to kill those who use the illegal letter.

People are tired of this,
They plead for the lift of this oppressive law.
People raise arms, time for peace is over
Water pistols at the ready to fight the killer robots
We desire freedom! Give us the letter!

Ozzy Majewski (14)
Newman Catholic College, Brent

ADVENTURE

(Haiku poetry)

To the large forest
Group of plants not the poorest
Creatures are flawless

Through the open air
Clear paths leading to somewhere
Dinosaurs beware

Wide open mountains
Positioned like football teams
As I skipped them through

Slipped through wide-ranged sea
As a wandering prey, sharks
Slithering like snakes

Climbing up mountains
With heavy sack on my back
Through the stubborn rocks

Walking up the peak
Pictured the environments
That were green and blue

Parachuting through
The clear air as the lands are
All smothered in green

Grounds blanketed by
Formed white icy crystals as
I tripped down through it.

Samuel Davis (14)
Newman Catholic College, Brent

LIPOGRAPH: NO LETTER H

Cybernetics in a mental state
Monstrosity in its weakest way
Escalating in a continuous state
An uprising, never again?

Menace its powerless appeal
Illustration of its own kind
Will it never end?

Won't it ever stop?
Will we suffer an extermination?
Maybe we will never persevere
No one will ever realise...

Can you recognise the aberration?
Everyone can exist
Some survive
Most will never know.

Simeon Bozilov (14)
Newman Catholic College, Brent

PEACE

Peace only comes only moments after tears,
Only once you have faced your fears
But there is a difference between
Being at peace and being alone,
There is a difference between
Being known and unknown
Everyone has had a sad moment in their life
Everyone has suffered and had strife
Inside us is an ocean of emotion
And sometimes we drown in it
We feel like we are having a fit
But here is some advice
You should always just be nice.

Ava Annis Klara Drew (12)
Sedgehill School, Lewisham

CHANGE

I hate how people change,
Nothing can ever stay the same,
Can't you remember the old days?
Like it was just yesterday,
Remember on the streets you used to say hey?
Now we're moving fast,
Now we're in two different lanes.

Why do we insult each other,
With the phrase 'being gay'?
Wasn't pride meant to be celebrated,
Motivated?
Now we use it in such a bad way.

All the racism truly makes me sick,
How we're hating on each other,
On the skin we're born with,
And all this drill music,
Is it all just a trick?
Killing one another,
'Cause of the town we're born in.

We need to stop the violence,
We need to stop the crime,
People walking round here,
Like killing people is life's biggest triumph.

I'm usually pretty good at putting on a mask,
I mean I do it all the time,
And if anyone ever suspects anything's wrong,
I shut them off with, "I'm fine."

But today I was really struggling,
And I couldn't fake another smile,
It's exhausting trying to keep up this ID,
And I don't want to live in denial.

But knowing it wasn't an option,
I braced myself for another day,
I could feel myself getting agitated,
Hoping it would go away.

Everything was going wrong,
I could feel myself about to burst,
Emotions rushing to the surface,
Preparing myself for the worst.

I could see them in the distance,
Smiling from afar,
What was wrong with me?
What was wrong with my resistance?

They made themselves over,
Like I wasn't a freak,
I saw the look in their eyes,
I felt like I was weak.

Next thing I remember,
My eyes were just flooding,
Telling them my whole story,
But yet, I don't worry.

Shannay
Sedgehill School, Lewisham

UNDERWATER

Being underwater is the only place
Where I can have peace
Without those hungry beasts
Watching me all the time
And as soon as I climb out the water into the sunshine
There is a crime
But when I go back underwater
I feel as fine
As I was from when I was in the water
Although I cannot breathe underwater
I feel as if it's my home
Now that's the end of my poem.

Javyn
Sedgehill School, Lewisham

STARS

I wish
so many things
to every star I see

no matter
how childish
it may be

I whisper
each desire of mine
so hopefully

I realise then
that no one would hear
my lonely little plea

but the stars above...
Still, all they do
is look at me.

Chardonnay Warner Hall (14)
Sedgehill School, Lewisham

A NEW PAGE

That smile
Which was gone a while
Moments, which kept me dreaming
Wondering and wishing
Beginning of the new chapter
Where there won't be a shatter.

Do you remember the summer day
When we held hands in May?

When we thanked the God above
For having each other to love
When the flowers start to bloom
You'll know I'll be coming soon.

I had stood on the street
Where we were supposed to meet.

For the final date
Which you told me to wait
Where we had debate
Now. You planted your feet
On my street.

For the first date
And that was a checkmate
In the future
We were a rumour

There was a noise
From our boys.

Ilinka Jevtovic (17)
Southfields Academy, Wandsworth

THE FUTURE

I trudged through the mud
It pulled at my ankles
We secured our laser guns to our backs
"Right lads, up to! March on!"
The only thing we had for comfort
Were ourselves and the memories of our families at home
If we ever got there.
I thought of my children, my wife and the smell of their
perfume.
My nose caught the stench
Of these thousands of men with rotting feet in wet boots.
We have been going like this for five months now.
When will it stop?
Then lasers shot over our heads.
We all cried like babies looking for milk.
It had all become a blur.
They were all dead.
No one. No one I tell you will survive World War Three.
Get ready for some roaring thunder and lightning.
Because it's coming for you.

Skyla Jane Robertson (11)
St James Senior Girls' School, Hammersmith

AN ODE TO FLOWERS

I get some from a flower stand
I bring them home and magnificently
Put them in my most precious vase
I place them on my kitchen table
They brighten up the room like a brush with paint,
The dull, dirty oak of the table
Is now colourful and has some hope,
Day after day I water them so
Care for them like my own
Like a prodigy they change my view of life
One day I come home, locking the door behind me
My heart excited as I will see them
Yet one is dying,
Crisping,
Drying,
Day after day they fall,
Fall,
Fall,
Like rain but dry, the brown petals fall to the table,
My hope getting lesser
My heart getting emptier
The brightness falls, the colour dries
And I inside die
The one thing I had, that I thought I'd never lose
That had some colour
Had left me

I crouch on the floor sobbing and screaming
My thoughts bestial
Then I look up and see a petal falling
Red like blood
It falls to the ground and my heart is once again found.

Stella Robinson (13)
St James Senior Girls' School, Hammersmith

THE COOKIE MONSTER

My mom leans in to kiss me goodnight
I lie in my bed till I hear a fright
Of a person wandering down the stairs
Opening the cookie jar to see what's there
I grab my kit
And prepare to hit
The monster stealing my cookies.

I stand in front of this monster with pride
Till I see what he's trying to hide
With long pointed fingers
He has nails that linger
On my last cookie.

I give him a whack
And he eventually falls back
Letting go of my last cookie
But then I see that I couldn't be dafter
As this disgusting, hairy monster is crying in laughter
Because what I thought was a monster is really...

My ginormous monster of a brother stealing my last cookie!

Hazel Galloway (12)
St James Senior Girls' School, Hammersmith

AUTUMN

Leaves spun down, falling slowly
Bare trees stood alone, whispering
Their branches freezing without leaves,
But I stood there without moving.

I stood against the maple tree, alone
Whipping winds hit me, cold
Scarlet and maroon leaves covered the path.

Squirrels scattered to get nuts
The birds nested against the bare branches
I watched the world go by
Against the maple tree

My country was at stake, fighting in the war
Out here, I didn't care about anything
But the trees whispering
The birds nesting in the trees
The squirrels collecting nuts
Standing against the maple tree.

Bea Wright (12)
St James Senior Girls' School, Hammersmith

THE RED ACROBAT

Apple-red fur reflects onto the snow-white stripes
that cover his scars.
The delicate detail of his face is undeniable.
Grasping a rough branch that hangs from the sky,
His tail sways side to side for balance.
Blood-red ears twitch in the breeze.
Dark mittened gloves hold tightly.
His face lifts up into the sky.
Reaching up to grab his prize.
Squeezing,
Oozing,
The essence pouring onto his plump paws.
He takes a chomp while getting splatters of goodness on his
silk fur.
Every bite is celestial
But the energetic
Acrobatic red panda
Always adores the tangy taste of ripe dragon fruit.

Gabriella Claire Pinheiro Boyle (12)
St James Senior Girls' School, Hammersmith

INNER FEELINGS

My feelings bottled up inside
Something I'm sick of trying to hide
My emotions whirling out of control
Cold and empty, including my soul
My heart tied up in chains, sore.
It was rotting my core.
I wish I could soundly sleep and never wake up
Until the day my feelings were all grown up
I walked to the mirror and looked at myself
Seeing a girl in need of help
My feelings were tearing my world in half
That is why they were bottled up in the past
Like the sun covered by the low-lying clouds
Is how my feelings hide from the crowd.

Alice Fay Raeburn (13)
St James Senior Girls' School, Hammersmith

WISHFUL ADVENTURE

I'm bored
Please give me an adventure
I'll do anything
Please, I'm bored
I don't mind if it's a trip to the moon
Or if it's an escaped animal from the zoo
Please, please, I'm bored
I don't care if it's diving in the Maldives
Or if it's chasing shark thieves
If it's a witch having a bad day
She'll soon be saying hooray
I can sail over the angry sky
Just so the moon will go by
The stars will chase me
But I'll run as fast as can be
Give me an adventure please.

Isabel Thomas (13)
St James Senior Girls' School, Hammersmith

FIRST DAY

Hands shaking
Head aching
Throat burning
Tummy churning.

The school gates stood in front of me,
As girls skipped in with glee.
I said goodbye to my dad,
As he kissed me and squeezed my hand.

Hands waving,
Head raving,
Throat tingling,
Tummy jingling.

I stepped outside into the rain
As relief washed over my brain.
The day was finally over,
As my dad picked me up in his Rover.

Isla Ivanovic (11)
St James Senior Girls' School, Hammersmith

I WONDER

I wonder what the future will be,
I wonder if I will be alive to see,
To see all the new technology we make,
To see if global warming is still at stake?

What if people have computer brains?
What if people don't have to use trains?
What if transport is now a thing in the past?
And now people just teleport to where they went last?
But to live in the future, all I'd need
Is lots and lots of whipped ice cream!

Alice Suppiah (12)
St James Senior Girls' School, Hammersmith

HAPPY PLACE

The rain splattered across the neglected ground,
My thoughts alone made a sound,
Shivers scurried up my arm,
The rain had revealed its charm,
Inside almost felt like a gale,
Trapped inside your head buzzing like hail
Bedraggled thoughts went round my cramped head,
I was melodramatic but I felt dead,
My worries inundated away, it was a relentless chase
You should have seen my face,
I had found my happy place.

Scarlett Jones (13)
St James Senior Girls' School, Hammersmith

THE CLOUDS

I feel sad but alive
Breathing with a broken lung
I feel I love but am not loved
I need something to make me... me.

Like someone to chat to at three in the morning
Someone to laugh with every day
Someone who understands me
And loves me for me.

I want to play in the clouds
I want to talk whilst the sun comes up
I want to play the piano with a crowd
I want to dance with the fairies.

Lula Packshaw (12)
St James Senior Girls' School, Hammersmith

THE FUTURE

Space and robots
Already here
As the future gets closer
And starts with a tear.

You shall never know when the end is near
Perhaps it's already here,
Because the future is just becoming clear.

We shall never know how the future starts,
And we shall never know how it shall end,
Because after all,
All we know

Is that the future comes and goes!

Dulcie Airey-Lawrence (11)
St James Senior Girls' School, Hammersmith

IN THE FOREST

A n adventure starts with an eerie forest.
D ark branches brush past my face.
V icious animals crowd around.
E xcitement has turned to fear.
N oises terrifying all around.
T rembling explorers frightened into frozen statues.
U nidentified shadows press in.
R unning wolves in the distance.
E very adventure has an end.

Anete Mottus (11)
St James Senior Girls' School, Hammersmith

IT'S NOW OR NEVER

Heart thumping, blood pumping
Core aching, body shaking
Fingertips throbbing,
Trying to push the rock out of the way,
Trying to set myself free from this treacherous flooded
cave...
My hairs prickling like thorns,
Panic rising becoming mountains in my mind,
If I don't get out soon I won't ever get out,
It's now or never.

Rose Brabyn (11)
St James Senior Girls' School, Hammersmith

DARK AND GLOOMY

(Haiku poetry)

I can't dry my tears
They flow like a river and
Well up in my lap.

This blood on my hands
Was it me or someone else
I scarred so deeply?

I am plummetting
Down a bottomless abyss;
An endless cycle.

Living on the streets
People strolling by with smiles
With my cries unheard.

Death in my bedroom
Destruction in my blanket
Sorrow in my bed.

My life is empty
Incomplete, a hollow husk
That cannot be filled.

Humans are toxic
Killing trees, other people
Tainting Earth with trash

Humans are greedy
We'll rob a bank, take a life
For numbered papers.

Caught in a vortex
Drowning in the foul waters
That is my conscience.

Omniscient, dark
Parent though we're consuming
Feeding on our fear.

The omnipresent
Gloom, consumes my broken soul
One's inner conscience.

Isolating me
Like an old empty vessel
Abandoning me.

A surreal feeling
Of ever showing kindness
Gratitude maybe?

Regardless of that,
Hatred and horror scatters,
Fulfilling my soul.

I try to escape
I try to run or to hide
But it is too late...

Praise Onye-Koller (11)
St Matthew Academy, Blackheath

DEPRESSION

I don't know if it's an obsession,
though it causes me depression,
it's aggression.
I don't know if they can help it
and there's no one to talk to,
they have no idea what I've gone through.
I wish I could yelp
I need help...
but if I do my nightmares will come true,
I need you.
Every time I feel as if I want to deliver
at that moment I feel a shiver.
I have been stressin' and guessin'
why me? Why depression?
End this traumatism please, I ask,
as I feel I need to hide behind a mask.
At last I tell someone but begin to cry
but they never believe and say, "What a lie."
When I feel as if I need to die
I say the scary words, goodbye.
Listen to this, it is my confession
This is the story of my depression.

Nickoyah Aaliyah Forrest (12)
St Matthew Academy, Blackheath

WHAT A CRUEL WORLD

The laughter of a child bullying another,
A little boy crying for his mother,
The robberies of a selfish man,
Armed terrorists shooting from a van
I think, what a cruel world.

The wars between two different lands,
Groups of people fighting over their own plans,
Fake friends backstabbing in backs,
While innocent people are being kidnapped in sacks,
I think again, what a cruel world.

The unfairness of cruel people,
The sadness of a mother's heart,
A group of people crying out for freedom,
The anger of a bad start,
What a cruel world.

I see the sorrow in many eyes,
The heavy rain falling through the skies,
The pain once another dies,
When time goes by,
What a cruel world.

Wendy Arthur-Forson (12)
St Matthew Academy, Blackheath

AN ODE TO LULU

Everyone loves pugs,
Because they all love hugs,
But if they get a cold,
Make them nice and snug.

They are soft and cuddly,
And they're really, really snuggly,
And they also look,
Very, very pugly.

My pug is really fat,
She likes to lie on her mat,
But the one thing that she hates
Is fluffy pussy cats.

She loves to go on walks
And she eats food with a fork,
And the only thing that I wish for,
Is that she could talk.

She can do lots of tricks,
But she doesn't like fetching sticks,
Instead she likes to be at home,
Giving me lots of licks.

I love you so much Lulu
You are very cuckoo

But I still love you
Even when you have a poo-poo!

Beth Chowdhury
St Matthew Academy, Blackheath

KILLER CLOWN

Beware the clown of death you should fear
For you don't know that death starts here
They'll give you a scare
Go near, I dare.
The clown of death has a bat, probably a cane
But all you'll know is that you've been played
They'll look you down, chase you around
Give you a pound, KO, knocked out.
They'll creep around,
Not even make a sound
And when you're out at night don't be too loud.
They're in abandoned places
You won't see faces
When they swing their bat in your face you'll taste it
But let's face it,
It's a killer clown
But just one day
We'll take every single one of them down.

Tabi Istvan Ajuyah-Valentine (12)
St Matthew Academy, Blackheath

LONDON

L ife and live - we live here, spend our lives here

O bserve - noticing all the great things we have and the great in some people

N ew - new things will pass you like people, money, homes, every day you'll find new

D ream big - people come here to start and make a career and a journey

O bjective - pursue your goal, find what you like then do it

N ever enough - always too much traffic every day.

I have a nice view, leaving me amused
It has so much traffic, leaving me confused
But busy transport leaves me to have queues
It has cold weather needing me to get cosy
We have good food, leaving me in a good mood.
London.

Kassandra Kamegni Kadji (12)
St Matthew Academy, Blackheath

FEAR

The main thing, a part of life
I really know this
And let me tell you why

Nightmares are a part of fear
In your dreams
So when you wake up it'll make you scream

Clowns are super scary
At least they're not scarier
Than Bloody Mary

When imagining her in my head
It makes me fear
I always worry at night if she'll appear

Death is fear for people
And is what
They worry about in life
It sometimes convinces
People to walk around
The streets with a knife

And that is fear
This is the end
Hope you enjoyed it and I'll see you again.

Janae Daley (12)
St Matthew Academy, Blackheath

THE FUTURE

The future of the UK
Nobody can see
Robots are gonna take over
Land
Sky
And sea.
Around schools you shall see
On the road you will be
The UK's doomed for you and me
Before you know
The world's for them,
They'll take our place
And soon we'll be dead
When we're asleep they'll appear
Then we shall run
Mortal fear!
People of the world all shall surrender
From clowns to cops
Our lives would be tender
Water's gonna go
And green gloop's gonna take over
Terror and fear
An event to remember.

D'Metri Ramator
St Matthew Academy, Blackheath

WHAT IS HAPPENING TO THE WORLD?

In the world today
There are a lot of things happening
People making big decisions
Which they don't know how to control

Theresa May handling Brexit
I don't think it's going very well
She needs to exit
Brussels rejection
Is a devastation

Donald Trump
The President of the United States
Causing trouble

Kim Jong-un
The North Korean guy
Sending missiles
To god knows where

I don't know
What's wrong with these people
But they need to fix up
To make the world great again.

Shemmy Abidemi Adepoju (13)
St Matthew Academy, Blackheath

THE TIGER IN MY LIVING ROOM

A little tiger in the jungle.
Silky pearl-white fur,
Deep sea aqua eyes,
Inky-black shaded tips.
She stalks her prey,
And strategises her hunt.
With razor-like sharp claws,
Muscular hind legs,
And a thirst for blood.
Low on the floor,
Behind a table or chair,
She pounces with mighty force.
It's pinned down,
The prey has no escape,
Not against this beast.
Once it is caught,
The pleased little tiger returns to her den.
Placing it down,
She devours her hunt,
This is the way she sees the world.

Iciar Aranda Lopez (11)
St Matthew Academy, Blackheath

SPOOKY HALLOWEEN NIGHT

It's very spooky on Halloween night,
The ghosts and goblins will give you a fright

Watch your back, don't be blind
If you're not careful, who knows what you'll find?

You might see things like little black bats,
Or you might see things like scary black cats.

On every entrance there's a pumpkin or two,
With their creepy grins smiling at you.

It's very spooky on Halloween night
The ghosts and goblins will give you a fright.

Nivithan Nageswaran (11)
St Matthew Academy, Blackheath

TO MY FAMILY

I love my family, I really do
I can't forget when I was two
I was so sick but they were there
I know they really do care.

My brother and sister are both very funny
I like them because they give me money
They sometimes bully me
I wish I could make them see.

My mum and dad are always getting on to me
But they never want to see
The good things that happen to me
But I know they really do love me.

I love my family, I really do.

Daniella Olusanya (12)
St Matthew Academy, Blackheath

MUM AND DAD

My mum and dad love me
They love me
Love me

My mum and dad care for me
They care for me
Care for me

My mum and dad are there for me
They are there for me
There for me

My mum and dad are the best
They are the best
The best

People don't have mums or dads
No mum
No dad

Together we can make a loving, happy family
A loving, happy family
Family.

D'Angelo Pinnock (11)
St Matthew Academy, Blackheath

ODE TO A MOCHA FRAPPUCINO

Oh! How we adore your sweetness
Creamy, crunchy and cold,
When Mum decides to treat us,
On the menu you stand out bold.
Your rich, dark coffee energises me,
Velvet chocolate sauce - sticky on my tongue,
Foamy white cream like a heavenly cloud
Oh! For a friendly frappucino
Why can't everybody see
That your refreshing, icy crystals are full of fun?
And when I have you in my hand
I feel proud.

Kaede Takeda (11)
St Matthew Academy, Blackheath

CORRIDOR

Down the door is just a corridor
Judging my life on how the walls just cave in
Breaking me in pieces
So I can't survive
Until the weekend
Back then just hatred
Now, I just wanna break them
Closing in on me, making me dream
That I was far away
'Cause I just wanna say
All I feel is pain
Making me float away
I just hate corridors
'Cause all they do
Is dictate.

Sami Ahmad (13)
St Matthew Academy, Blackheath

NATURE/AUTUMN

The leaves swing from the trees
From the autumn bliss.
I wonder why they give me a leafy kiss?
I love when leaves make a crunchy sound.
When they swing from the tree
And go to the ground.
The leaves change colour
Like yellow, orange and red.
In the autumn,
Animals are getting ready to go to bed.

Marvel Katchisicho Ozorka (12)
St Matthew Academy, Blackheath

KNIVES

Knife crimes kill loads of people
It is a dangerous weapon
It can kill
People crying and dying
And it's more in London
Gang-related
People turning a blind eye to this behaviour
People need to stop this
'Cause this is affecting adolescents on the road
Don't you question this?

Ashley Thomas (11)
St Matthew Academy, Blackheath

THE SPACE

The space, so big...
I am a spacecraft pilot
Going up the ladder
I entered the spacecraft, wow!
Nine, eight, seven, six,
Five, four, three, two, one... launch
... And the rocket flew.

Hugo Hernandez Muelas (13)
St Matthew Academy, Blackheath

WHERE'S THE ESCAPER?

Watching very closely
Standing hardly breathing
Slinking and gliding like a rat
On the railings it's clinging
But there for its prey it sat!

Kavin Premkumar (12)
St Matthew Academy, Blackheath

TRUE BEAUTY

It is true there is beauty in the complex,
The ocean and its inhabitants are intricate.
The details immaculate.
The leaves on a tree,
Every single thing has a purpose.
But there is also beauty in simplicity;
A white gown, no matter how simple it is,
Is still beautiful
A swan, even though it is plain,
Is considered a creature of grace.
A black raven, even though it is common,
Is still interesting and wonderful in its own way.
Likewise, people are the same.
Some are eagles and others are swans.
A peacock is not extraordinary in the same way as an
albatross.
You are perfect as you are,
And no one is beautiful in the same way as you.

Mary Mullagiri (14)
Thames Christian School, Clapham

ADVENTURE AWAITS

Adventure is out there, it awaits,
It gives lots of life updates,
Adventure awaits, it is out there,
I truly love adventures, but where?

Australia is a place to go,
To get outside and find new mojo,
I enjoy Australia 'cause I lived there,
I also truly love the Australian animals as some are rare.

So many choices of adventure here,
If you go hiking you need the proper gear,
Biking is exceptionally good on warm weeks,
Especially going down the precipitous peaks.

New Zealand is a place to go
To see unique animals also,
I was born in their August winter,
The birthplace of the greatest rugby players.

Locals will give high-quality accommodation
The country is well known for lamb, but they offer the best chicken
Bungee jumping is the best activity
When I bungee jumped I smiled with glee.

Adventure is out there, it awaits,
Helps you to understand your fates,

Adventure awaits, it is out there,
I truly love the adventure air.

Bailey Bright (13)
Thames Christian School, Clapham

TWO TOWERS

Two twins who have grown
Two twins both well known

Two twins standing tall
Two twins as they fall

Two twins when they drop
Two twins when life stops

Two twins that are firm
Two twins that have burned

Two twins in the end
Two twins that descend

Two twins without rust
Two twins left to dust

Two twins who have grown
One plane left alone

One plane flies around
One plane so near

One plane in the ground
One plane full of fear

One plane that shoots like a dart
One plane in a dash

One plane that has hearts
One plane that will crash

One plane that will glide
One plane that will soar

No place left to hide
The twins on the floor.

Elijah Booth (15)
Thames Christian School, Clapham

SONNET TO MY MOTHER

She is the sun's scintillating strong beam
against the darkness of night's eerie cloak,
the temperate noise from a running stream
the grand, great presence of a chestnut oak.
Wherever she goes tenderness follows
and dances and prances, enchanting me.
Caught in her kindness I'm fully swallowed
like bright sparkling stars in the galaxy.
She helped me through tough times and I stood tall,
when people said I can't she said I can,
she helps me to get up each time I fall,
raising a young boy to a grown-up man.
My dear mum, I thank you for what you do,
my love for you is heartfelt, deep and true.

Max McFarlane (13)
Thames Christian School, Clapham

TREE

Calm, harmonious, serene
Radiant rays of summer come between
Light grey months, of the destroyer let it not be seen
Yet I have seen it and it sits on top, a crown on a queen
Simple but captivating - the beauty of the Japanese
Delicately dancing in a breeze, I unfreeze
Champagne pink grass, I was on my knees
A silhouette of women in a tree.
Cordial foreigners' glee
The glowing incense of cream and pollen
And the dainty curves of pink have fallen.
You must all see the beauty of the tree.

Tsion Tafari (13)
Thames Christian School, Clapham

RHYME CRIME

There was once crime
In this world of rhyme
In this place where there was no time
Everyone swished around
Like lush slushies
Running around with no boundaries
This unboundedness annoyed criminals
The unboundedness made a bind for them
Sadly but gladly the criminals went away
But not forever, for they still endeavoured to raid the daily parade
This parade occurred in the day
When the crime started to go into play.

Micah Donnan (14)
Thames Christian School, Clapham

TOAST

Toast is like a small patch of desert
Like a buttered slice of sunshine
Like the bristles on a man's stubbled chin.
Toast is as crisp as autumn leaves
As creamy as cappucino
As burnt as bark
As glittery as gold
Toast is toast.

Leilani Champagnie (13)
Thames Christian School, Clapham

THE WORDS OF WW2

The words of war,
Are the ones who hypnotise
Decent, hard-working people,
Into hatred and despise.

The words of war,
Are the ones that dig fear
Into every living man,
Enough to make his humanity disappear.

The words of war,
Are the reason that the bombs
Blew up the families,
Who believed in the cause.

The words of war
Are the ones that make people think that it's okay
To send their friends and neighbours to their deaths,
And stone them on the way.

The words of war,
The words of death,
The words of greed,
And the words of theft.

Those are the words of war,
The words that kill the ones who reject

That want to steal the lives
Of their lifelong friends.

Chelsea Nicole Findley (13)

The Ellen Wilkinson School For Girls, Acton

SPEAK MY MIND

Words.
I write them, I speak them, I read them, I think them.
So many thoughts that go unsaid,
Whirling around and around in my head.
If my thoughts were an ocean,
I'd be drowning,
If my thoughts were light,
I'd be blinded,
But my thoughts aren't an ocean,
My thoughts aren't light,
My thoughts are lost in an endless fight.
A fight to be heard, a fight to stay in,
It's staying in that always wins.
My thoughts are fear, the courage I can't find
The courage I need
To speak my mind.

Terriesia Blackstock (13)
The Ellen Wilkinson School For Girls, Acton

192

THE FALLEN ANGEL

His eyes are red
His wings are spread
Welcoming you into his gorgeous arms
He is darkness, but also a charm.
A fallen angel he is
Dragging darkness from evil's hands into his.
Ruling the world is his desire
His passion is to play with fire
His appearance will attract you
His betrayal will break you.
He is an immortal
That can't cross the holy portal
He is a diamond that has been pearled
But finish him, or the world he will.

Raisa Khan Ahmed (13)
The Ellen Wilkinson School For Girls, Acton

WHEN WILL IT BE?

Today or tomorrow
You may feel the sorrow

Will you make the correct choice?
Will you use the right voice?
Will you know when you will die?
Will you need to tell a lie?

The future is a second, minute, hour, day, week, month away
There is no yesterday.

The past is history
You will choose your story.

There are many days ahead
Will you be the one who's led?

When will it be?

Ada Ulusoy (13)
The Ellen Wilkinson School For Girls, Acton

HOUSE DIVIDED BY LOVE

The
Light of two
Hearts spread apart
Leaving me in the dark.

I never felt this way before
Until you slammed the door

Rain against the windowpane
It's running down, I feel ashamed.

My fault or is it yours?
I know we both have our flaws
Flaws, flaws, floors.

Our love had no limits
No ceiling to it.

The shards of glass fell from the sky
All I needed was a lullaby.

To put me to sleep
In these cold bedsheets

In my dreams our love is stable
But then you left your ring on the bedside table.

Aisha Creary (15) & Lara Marah (15)
The Royal Docks Community School, Newham

SYNTHETIC

Society, we all want to change *society*,
Yet how can we change *society*
When we are constantly moulding ourselves to fit its vision?
Is this not hypocrisy?

We always drag others through the dirt, for what?
A miniscule chance to reach the top,
Ambition is our folly.

It's the twenty-first century,
We're all for equality!
But the wage gap still exists,
Three cheers for the feminists!

Boys, grown men, don't cry,
A natural emotion that falls from each eye,
Let's not forget what happened to that guy,
They gave him a reason to cry.

What a wonderful caricature of our golden age,
Smear your blood on the page,
Sell your soul,
To gain it all.

I'm angry,
Look at what we claim to be,
The best generation - so entitled are we,
Social media: a joy, an enemy,

Simply a warped version of reality,
Society dictating who we should be.

We're just as bad as the next,
Moulding ourselves until we break,
Maybe then we'll be more real,
Not fake.

Mahek Rabbani (14)
The Royal Docks Community School, Newham

FEELINGS POEM

Love the people
Love is a feeling
Love gives the power in life
It helps you to survive
You are the love of my life
I am sorry that I can't help you
I'm sorry that I can't talk to you every day
I'm sorry for every argument we got into
However
I'm happy that we met
I'm happy that we spent a lot of time together
I'm happy that we became friends
I'm happy for having the chance to know you
I'm happy for all the good times we shared
To know that you're happy will make me even happier.

Adeil Glulam (11)
The Royal Docks Community School, Newham

SORROW'S LIFE CYCLE

There is no pain without agony
Nor is there agony without pain
This poem will make your life drain
Those two members of the devil's heart
Will rip your life apart.
Tear, tear, tear!
Until your soul can no longer bear
You see your life rush past your eyes
Then you realise your life is all lies
When the last tear comes
All that you have will be gone
This goes on and on
For the rest of your days
And there it lies...

Sabina Memia (11)
The Royal Docks Community School, Newham

THE FUTURE

The future is uncertain
Grab all the present moments you can contain
Aren't we worried too much about the future?
Because to live for others is the choice of nature
Take care of the planet
Each one of us has a talent
Find it if you haven't
Use it in a useful way
It can bring joy to each new day
Be careful what you do
'Cause you might regret it
Later I bet
Life is like a test
Live your life to the best.

Bianca Constantin (11)
The Royal Docks Community School, Newham

THE FUTURE

Cars on the floor,
Not anymore.
People wear crazy stuff,
Because of the future.
Houses are shaped a new way,
Dogs now have nutty fur coats.
Doctor Who, that's old news.
New stuff everywhere,
Even robots now are here.

Bailey Scott-Fisher (11)
The Royal Docks Community School, Newham

TO THE LOST

The sound of the gunfire filled my head
Boom! Boom! Boom!
The sound of the bombings filled me with dread
Boom! Boom!
More blood spread
If only this torture would come to an end
If only this war would be over
If only the people hadn't thought of such a pernicious idea
If only the people were not so fallacious.

Surrender or die!
Blood and more blood
Torture and more torture
Pain and more pain
Loss and more loss.

The year is 1918, the war is over
The year is 2018
100 years ago the war came to an end.

To the lost, two minutes' silence for the dead
To the lost, I thought of the battlefields, of when they were red
Red, not of the poppies, but of the blood of the dead
To the lost, two minutes' silence for the dead
To the lost, 'lest we forget'.

Chloe Yagoub Arostegui (12)
Ursuline High School, Wimbledon

SEASON SONNET

In autumn the leaves are golden and brown
The farmers begin to harvest their crops
November the fifth, fireworks light up the sky
We dress up to scare on Halloween night.

In the cold of winter we light our fires
We prepare for Christmas with our families
Snowflakes fall from the freezing cold blue skies
And celebrate and have fun on New Year's.

In spring the pretty flowers are blooming
Baby lambs are born throughout the new season
The trees are sprouting lovely green new leaves
And the sun begins to shine once again.

The sky is blue and the sun is blazing
The bees are buzzing around the nice flowers
The sea is turquoise and full of bright fish
The golden sand runs through your fingertips.

Blue skies in summer, dark clouds in winter
Baby lambs in spring, autumn leaves splinter.

Eimear Fehily (13)
Ursuline High School, Wimbledon

THE MAIN QUESTION

Life can be:
Amazing
Praising
Boring,
Or even soaring!
Life can make you feel
Out of the blue,
Starting anew
But do people even think?
Even at the second when they blink,
What does life even mean?

It may be irrelevant,
But I can choose that it's evident!
To let my people know,
It's something I want to show.

Why are we here?
Is time's ending near?
Did dinosaurs exist?
Or is God in our midst?

They say, "Don't think too far!"
"It'll leave you with a scar!"
They say that I'm too young,
To question with such a tongue.

But! I believe in myself,
To know what's on the top of that shelf,
To speak loud and clear,
To stand with no fear...

Chantal Badayos (12)
Ursuline High School, Wimbledon

THE MOUSE

Once upon a time, not long ago
There was a mouse who had just left his humble abode
He was craving for hunger, yearning for thirst
But there was a feeling inside that was about to burst

While searching pantries in every house
Something was nibbling inside of him - just like a mouse.
Suddenly a human bounded in and gazed upon the disarraying sight
"A rat! A rat! What a harrowing fright!"
He stood there in shock before running away
And the remark still offends him to this day.

While the rodent turned kitchens upside down
Something horrible happened which turned his life around
While he was confined in a trap he finally realised
He was only a mouse, this was changed by no cry.

Gemma Sweeney (12)
Ursuline High School, Wimbledon

LOVE IS LOVE

Love is like a sugary strawberry lace
It can be traced moments after digestion
It has a sweet taste
Losing love is like a punch in the face
Don't let it go to waste.

Love is like a silky blue sea
It can make you feel extremely happy
It brings joy flooding through us
Like a child's first time at Toys 'R' Us.

Love is like an ice cream
It sometimes makes us scream
It isn't about me, me, me
Love is in sickness and in health
It isn't just about wealth
Love can't be pulled off a bookshelf
It can look after itself
Nurse it from its seed
Don't let it become a stray weed.

Love is love.

Rosemary Chiamaka Ukaha (12)
Ursuline High School, Wimbledon

NO ONE KNOWS

No one knows what it's like to hide,
No one knows the agonies inside.
When all you see is black and red,
You never know what horrors lie ahead.

Under the smile painted on my face,
You have no idea about my darkened place.
Where the trees don't sway and no flowers grow.
Where it's always cold and wind does blow.

No one can see me, no one can know,
It's always cold but never snow.
And with the horrors I face alone,
My heart turns black and then to stone.

No one knows how to comfort me,
I'm drowning in my own black sea.
If only someone can hear my cries,
Before a part of me silently dies.

Sophia Theresa Libera-Bennett (12)
Ursuline High School, Wimbledon

BLACK BEAUTY

Skin all black, silky and smooth
Breathing all slow then suddenly it moved
Arriving slowly, shoes all shiny
Body so elegant and movements so tiny.

Ears so soft and eyes a deep brown
Oh sight so deep and pupils so round
Hearing so sharp but the background very dark
Pouncing up and down, feeling as proud as a lark.

Feeling so sad wishing for hope
I can't bear the feeling, I just can't cope
Black as night, I just can't think
I'm watching it sip and drink and drink.

Just guess what this is
An amazing creature
Black Beauty, that's it
A hero full of features.

Sia Bart (12)
Ursuline High School, Wimbledon

BULLYING

We are constantly
Brought under ourselves
Calling out through
Our muted voices
We are drowned in a pool
Of loneliness as we are
Pinched by fallacious rumours,
Pernicious comments
And invective insults.

Crypted codes circle
Our infected minds
As the epidemic slowly spreads
Like butter into the community
Nevertheless, the journey continues
As we plough through the
Deep earth in shame.

But yet again
We fall into that dark hole
Which we try so hard to stay out of
Yet, however hard we try,
It feels so familiar to us.

Until we cannot come out.

Sophie Jeanine Zirps (13)
Ursuline High School, Wimbledon

INSIDE OF ME

I stood there in the utter dark
Waiting for something or someone to come
To gobble me up like a shark
Nobody will come, not even my mum.

I am absolutely alone
Loneliness and fear is a crashing storm
I cannot even cry or moan
I wish to be completely safe and warm.

Shadows approach me in the night
Goosebumps come and bite all over my skin
This is too hard to have a fight
In this situation you cannot win.

Don't ever try to hide or run
It will not help but will make it all worse
In this case you cannot have fun
This is an absolute and total curse.

Lana Kirstie Howlett (12)
Ursuline High School, Wimbledon

WHAT IS LOVE?

Love, what is love?
Love is cruel
An erupting volcano trying to escape
Love is pernicious
Love is a burning rage
Love, what is love?
Love is cruel.

Love, what is love?
Love is non-existent
A distant dream perched above
Love is a drug we are addicted to
Love is a black hole
Love, what is love?
Love is non-existent.

Love, what is love?
Love is a box of chocolates
You never know what you'll get
Love is a smile upon one's face
Love is the taste of pizza
Love, what is love?
Love is a box of chocolates.

Izabella Mia Dudziec-Mabasi (13)
Ursuline High School, Wimbledon

HALLOWEEN

Witches, vampires, devils and zombies
This is what Halloween's about
If you're ready for Halloween give me a cheer
For I can see it crystal clear
Decorating the house is definitely the best
The pumpkins lit up make a wonderful effect
The demons start to shout
Halloween has come, I can see it about.

In the middle of the night we leave the house
We see our friends to get some sweets
We walk the streets to trick or treat
Eat your sweets, take a seat
The next day we are all wanting more
It comes next year, but we can just go to the store.

Carolina Agulhas Goncalves (13)
Ursuline High School, Wimbledon

SANDWICHIFRY

I woke up this morning,
Wondering what's for lunch.
Still dozy and yawning,
Exultant at my munch.

But then I realised
Oh deary me!
My mind was capsized
By the art of sandwichifry!

Medium or large?
My brain was in charge.
Fish, veg or meat?
I just need to eat!

Butter or no butter?
Where's my cheese cutter?

Wait, cream or cheese?
Ouch, my tummy!

Triangular or square?
I really couldn't care!

Please,
Just make me a sandwich.

Siena Winstone (13)
Ursuline High School, Wimbledon

OMINOUS FIGURE WHO JUST LURKS AROUND

Ominous figure slinking in the wood,
All of you hidden behind that hood,
Too scared to be seen and too scared to be found,
You are just a meaningless figure who lurks around.

All of your beauty and all of your grace,
Hidden behind that dark, dark face,
You always wander near and away,
I see you night by night and day by day.

But who are you, I don't know,
Maybe friend or maybe foe,
You're a shadow who makes no sound,
You are just a meaningless figure who lurks around.

Maya Carla Staron (12)
Ursuline High School, Wimbledon

CANCER

Cancer: the heart shatterer
Takes away the things that matter
The shedder of tears
A sickening pit of fear
Screaming, shouting, sobbing, crying
Fear, tears, hiding, lying.

Cancer: pernicious
No more time to be ambitious
Treacherous torture in a word
Shivers in spines to be lured
One day the smile is there
The next you couldn't care.

The last goodbyes
The falling tears
The closing eyes
The confirmed fears

The battle's up
Silence.

Ella Delaney (12)
Ursuline High School, Wimbledon

LIFE IS MAKE-BELIEVE

D reamy people sit around, joyful as can be,

I ntoxicated faces sit behind their screens, believing everything they see,

C aptivated by their phones, unable to be free,

T rapped in the simulation of life, just like you and me,

A ssailment from technology keeps us all contained,

T orturing our souls, leaving us forever pained,

I solation, depression, sadness, despair,

O ppose me if you want - but I will always be there,

N eglected but true.

Jessica Mae Reeves (12)
Ursuline High School, Wimbledon

BOTTLED UP INSIDE

My feelings shut away inside
Like a vault whose key is lost
No one can find a way in
Not even I...

They're eating away at me
Screaming to get out
I can't let them free
What is happening to me?

My mind being clouded
Like a foggy day
I feel like a hostage
Being taken away.

No one can see what's happening
Stone-faced on the outside
I'll be shunned if I show how I feel
But I won't let them be taken away.

Katie Pryor (12)
Ursuline High School, Wimbledon

WHO ARE THE MONSTERS?

Full of hate,
Covered in guilt.
Dripping with shame,
Humans are the real monsters.

They start a fight,
Such as pollution.
Wake up at day and sleep at night,
Humans are the real monsters.

Dark, dark souls
Hearts made of stone.
Evil are their goals,
Humans are the real monsters.

As they creep behind the beds,
Rocking babies to sleep, humming.
But their eyes fill with dread,
Realising humans are the real monsters.

Masha Nesterenko (12)
Ursuline High School, Wimbledon

THE INNER ME...

You judge me and I judge you
I judge me and you judge you
We aren't just captive to each other's approval
But for our own good signal
Our own opinions are dangerous
So we must stay courageous
We poison ourselves with envy
Even if we are being friendly
Social expectations are rising
But our own disapproval is thriving
We return to the primitive
But is that really definitive?
If skin deep beauty be,
Can we see the inner me?

Eirinn Furey (13)
Ursuline High School, Wimbledon

FEELINGS

Happy, sad, angry, confused
Cheerful, downcast, irate, amused
What are these feelings inside my head?
I wish they would go, I could choose instead!

How did they get there?
When will they go?
The answer to this I do not know.
Sometimes I feel like I am touching the sky
And other days I really just don't want to try.

I can't help my feelings
However I may try
My feelings will spread their wings
Like a butterfly.

Anna Banks (12)
Ursuline High School, Wimbledon

DREAMS

A dream can make you happy,
A dream can make you sad.
Where knights are fighting battles,
Or elves are fooling around.
You meet your favourite pop star,
Or parachute down to Earth.
Dreams can turn into nightmares,
You will witness something evil.
Something that wakes you up,
Like creeping around a haunted house
Or a ghost shouting boo
Dreams can make you cry
Dreams can make you laugh
Look at that dragon flying by!

Grace Stanger (12)
Ursuline High School, Wimbledon

MONSTERS INSIDE MY HEAD

I told you I wanted to go
A monster's taking over my brain
'Cause you don't really know
What it's like to feel this pain

There's a demon inside my head
Who tells me what to do
It's worse than the one under my bed
Who normally comes out of the blue.

People think it's my imagination
But it was here from the start
I'm yelling out in desperation
It's tearing me apart.

Franchesca Sales Brosas (13)
Ursuline High School, Wimbledon

FAKE FRIENDS

The beginning of the year
May have been full of fear
Yet once friends are made
All your fears fade...

Friends are caring and kind
That's why they are hard to find
Yet be careful, some may be fake
From a big star it turns into a flake
Leaving you behind and making you sad
Making you cry and go mad
You try to get back, your relationship is cracking
But it doesn't work as their friendship is lacking.

Martyna Mackow (12)

Ursuline High School, Wimbledon

I'M SLIPPING INTO THE DEEP END

I'm slipping into the deep end
Death could be an option
Just around the bend
Struggling for air
Yet no one cares.

Trying to break free
Trying to just be me
You can hide it with a smile
Or have a laugh for a while.

But it comes back
The fear, the pain, the happiness I lack
I'm still slipping into the deep end
Who knows, depression could be a new trend.

Freya Smith (12)
Ursuline High School, Wimbledon

THE SADNESS OF DEATH

Misery and heartache
Dark and deep

Buried six feet under
With no heartbeat

Your life is gone
No one is left

You're alone in the dark
With many regrets

Your soul is gone
Your body left
With flies buzzing on your chest

Screams and cries echo in my head
You think, *why did I let my dreams
Take me to rest?*

Janaya Prempeh-Maitland (12)
Ursuline High School, Wimbledon

LOVE

Love is beauty
A part of your life
You have to accept it
There is no fight.

Love is a rose
It blossoms until it's best
It nourishes and grows
Until it's put to rest.

Love is the devil
It breaks your heart
It tears you up
You fall apart.

Love is poison
You're under its spell
You do what it says
Or go to hell.

Cliona O'Brien (12)
Ursuline High School, Wimbledon

IT'S ALL UP TO US

I wonder what it's like in the future
Will there be flying cars?
Or will the world come to an end?
It's all up to us.

Will there be humans?
Or will we become extinct?
Will robots take over the world?
It's all up to us.

Will we find cures for all diseases?
Or will there never be a cure?
Will the NHS still exist?
It's all up to us.

Amelia Brewster (12)
Ursuline High School, Wimbledon

HER LAST LETTER

Tears ran down his cheek
As he read the last words she wrote,
The paper was stained with blood and fear,
Also with the ink that wrote,
'I know I will never see you,
I know that I will die,
Do not worry about me anymore,
I'm really not alone,
Things are starting to fade,
No, I'm not alone dear,
Please don't be afraid'.

Isabella Brown (12)
Ursuline High School, Wimbledon

INNER BEAUTY COMES FROM WITHIN

I nner beauty comes from within
N ever doubt your beauty
N ever doubt yourself
E verything within you
R eminds me of beauty

B eauty is power
E veryone's a flower
A beautiful creation
U ntil it blooms
T en feet tall
Y ou'll realise you are beautiful.

Natalia Pasinska (13)
Ursuline High School, Wimbledon

IT'S HALLOWEEN

It's Halloween,
It's Halloween,
The bats come out,
The cats come out

Pumpkins are carved
Witches are scarred
Demons laugh and whisper
Beware or get a blister.

Full of cheer we knock on doors,
Taking sweets we hear some roars
Once a year, it's a free for all
Trick or treat until next fall.

Rukevwe Agofure (12)
Ursuline High School, Wimbledon

FEELINGS

Anger, fear, love, joy
Whether it's felt by a girl or boy
Different levels, different floors,
Each one opening up different doors.

If it is strong or if it is weak,
If we hold it in or let it leak
Each one showing a different effect
Fear of loss or fear of debt.

Liliana Carlon (12)
Ursuline High School, Wimbledon

A WAVE OF EMOTIONS

Sadness is like a titanic wave
Engulfing you in a gigantic wave
Grabbing you from behind
Taking your soul
Stealing your heart
And ruining your goals

Suddenly your mood has changed
From a pernicious thought
To a bundle of joy
Now
A wave of happiness.

Erin Andrew (13)
Ursuline High School, Wimbledon

THE BEAUTY WITHIN

A beauty that comes from within
Is a beauty that age cannot wrinkle
Nor be distracted by a pimple.
It is more than a reflection
It is a conception
It is a radiant smile
It is a form of a flower
The hidden oasis in every desert
The voice of true power!

Florence Conrad (12)
Ursuline High School, Wimbledon

BAKED BEAN LABELS ON COLD TUNA TINS

In most cases
We misconceive
Baked bean labels on cold tuna tins

If something doesn't
Seem quite right
A label is not far behind

Don't feel alone
It's not you putting
Baked bean labels on cold tuna tins.

Sofia Maya Ferreiro (12)
Ursuline High School, Wimbledon

HOSTAGE

Imprisoned like a hostage
As the captor and the captive
Mind of ice
But heart of gold

The walls collapse
Closing you inside
Panic
Trapped
Breathe
Gone.

Ivie Omorogiuwa (13)
Ursuline High School, Wimbledon

LOVE, PAIN, ANGER

(A haiku)

Love is forever
Pain is feeling trapped, lonely,
Anger defines you.

Lara Recordon (12)

Ursuline High School, Wimbledon

STARSHIP

Through the inky unknown
The starship floats
Ploughing alone
Into the deep emptiness of space
Their destination: a distant grain of light
Almost drowned by the desolation
Of its surroundings.

The crew guide the ship on
Into the future
With their old existence washed away
And their new one yet to be forged
They have crossed one threshold
But are far off the next.

Despite their struggles
They stick together
Not out of want
But out of need
The road behind them
No longer is there
The road ahead
Is mottled with the unknown.

But the starship floats on
Unabating, into the deep
In search of light

In search of warmth
The crew too continue
Faith yokes them together
All united in search
Of that tiny grain of light.

Ben Heyes (13)
Westminster School, Westminster

A STARSHIP

The starship breaches the clouds,
Burning with the fire of knowledge
It flies on silver wings, laden with discoveries
Laden with curiosity and hope.

The starship dips lower,
Burning with the fire of wisdom
It circles like a great bird, bearing peace and love
Raining its gifts down upon the Earth.

The starship lands, roaring with the divine inferno of war
It brings ash and blood, crushing those who stand in its way
Stretching its titanium wings over the world
Raising its mighty, bloody head.

The starship burns into my eyes like a second sun
As the door to the new world opens.

Arthur Boyce-Rodgers (14)
Westminster School, Westminster

THE STARSHIP

Encapsulated
my trajectory decided
by them
on the way
apparently
to the stars
"Be who you
want to be,"
they say
in their
icy tenderness

sitting on the
pews
"We are all made in
God's image,"
mumbles
the priest as
people grin
and grimace
knowing full
well that we
are being
conformed into
aimless
human beings.

Baruch Lulsegged MacGregor (14)
Westminster School, Westminster

Young Writers Est. 1991

YOUNG WRITERS
INFORMATION

We hope you have enjoyed reading this book – and that you will continue to in the coming years.

If you're a young writer who enjoys reading and creative writing, or the parent of an enthusiastic poet or story writer, do visit our website **www.youngwriters.co.uk**. Here you will find free competitions, workshops and games, as well as recommended reads, a poetry glossary and our blog. There's lots to keep budding writers motivated to write!

If you would like to order further copies of this book, or any of our other titles, then please give us a call or visit **www.youngwriters.co.uk**.

Young Writers
Remus House
Coltsfoot Drive
Peterborough
PE2 9BF
(01733) 890066
info@youngwriters.co.uk

Join in the conversation!
Tips, news, giveaways and much more!

YoungWritersUK   **@YoungWritersCW**